DARK

✠ AND HURRYING ✠

DAYS

MENZIES'
1941 DIARY

Edited by A.W. Martin
and Patsy Hardy

NATIONAL LIBRARY OF AUSTRALIA

National Library of Australia Cataloguing-in-Publication entry

Menzies, Sir Robert, 1894–1978.
  Dark and hurrying days : Menzies' 1941 diary.

  Includes index.
  ISBN 0 642 19285 5.

  1. Menzies, Sir Robert, 1894–1978—Diaries. 2. Prime ministers—
  Australia—Diaries. 3. World War, 1939–1945—Australia.
  4. World War, 1939–1945—Great Britain. I. Martin, A.W.
  (Allan William), 1926– . II. Hardy, Patsy. III. National
  Library of Australia.

994.042092

Publications Manager: Margaret Chalker
Publisher's editor: Carol Miller
Designer: Julia Reingold
Indexer: Alan Walker

Printed by Goanna Press, Canberra

FOREWORD

The Diary kept by the Australian Prime Minister, R.G. Menzies, during his wartime visit to England in 1941 is held in the National Library of Australia as part of the extensive collection of the Papers of Sir Robert Menzies. The Diary deals with a critical period in the history of the Second World War from 24 January 1941 when Menzies left Australia to his return on 24 May. In it, Menzies recorded observations on his experiences, the people he met and his own thoughts and feelings. The Diary offers an interesting and valuable insight into Menzies', and Australia's, relationship with Britain at a time of world crisis.

Allan Martin and Patsy Hardy, the joint editors of this published edition of R.G. Menzies' 1941 Diary, have provided a skilled and highly informed assessment of its historical significance. Their work draws heavily on the research they have done for the first volume of Dr Martin's biography of Sir Robert Menzies recently published by Melbourne University Press.

The Papers of Sir Robert Menzies are held in the National Library with other collections of personal papers of distinguished national figures. These materials constitute an important part of Australia's documentary heritage and provide a rich source for research and scholarship in many aspects of Australian life. Through its publications program, the National Library is pleased to ensure that a wider public, both in Australia and overseas, has access to this highly personal wartime record of one of Australia's major historical figures.

Warren Horton
Director-General
National Library of Australia

CONTENTS

'*Menzies, Australian Prime Minister abroad, assiduously films his experiences for family consumption —the aftermath of air raids, the historic monuments and stately homes, and, most importantly, the powerful political and social figures he meets.*' (AWM 7036)

His film provides an interesting supplement to the Diary and selected stills have been reproduced in this book (identified as 'Menzies Film').

Biographical Note

Robert Gordon Menzies was born in 1894 at Jeparit, in Victoria, the third son of a country storekeeper. A scholarship boy throughout, Menzies was educated at Grenville College, Ballarat, and at Wesley College, Melbourne, and studied Law at the University of Melbourne. He subsequently established a thriving barrister's practice in Melbourne, taking silk in 1929. In 1928 he was successful at a by-election for East Yarra Province in the Legislative Council of Victoria. At the general election of 1929 he transferred to the State's Legislative Assembly, winning the Nunawading seat. In 1932, at the fall of the Hogan Labor Government, Menzies became Attorney-General and Minister for Railways in the Nationalist Ministry formed by Sir Stanley Argyle.

Menzies was meantime one of a group responsible for establishing in 1931 the United Australia Party (UAP) to oppose the Depression policies of James Scullin's ruling Commonwealth Labor Government, and for persuading Joseph Lyons, once Scullin's Treasurer, to take the new party's leadership. Lyons won the 1932 federal election and became Prime Minister. In 1934 Menzies took the Kooyong seat for the House of Representatives and transferred to federal politics, becoming Lyons' Attorney-General. On Lyons' death in 1939 Menzies was elected by a narrow majority leader of the UAP, and therefore Prime Minister. After the outbreak of the Second World War he remained wartime Prime Minister for two years, until forced by his own party, in 1941, to resign the leadership.

The UAP collapsed at the general election of 1943 and Menzies was subsequently chief architect of a new Liberal Party which opposed the wartime and immediately post-war governments of John Curtin and Ben Chifley. The Liberals won the 1949 election and Menzies again became Prime Minister, holding this position for a record period until 1966, when he retired voluntarily at the age of seventy-two. He had been knighted in 1963, and after retirement was chosen by the British Government as Churchill's successor to the honorary post of Lord Warden of the Cinque Ports in 1965. Robert Menzies died in 1978.

Menzies' 1941 Diary: three plain-covered exercise books, with daily entries pencilled in Menzies' firm and lucid hand. (Menzies Papers)

PREFACE

The decision of the National Library of Australia to publish, in full, Menzies' Diary account of his visit to wartime England in 1941 is to be applauded. The Diary is an item in the Sir Robert Menzies Papers held in the manuscript collection of the Library. The original, written in pencil, is beginning to suffer from frequent use by research workers and it is essential that it be reproduced for the purpose of preservation. That the form of reproduction should be such as will make the Diary widely accessible is highly desirable. It is a document of great intrinsic interest, likely to appeal to a broad audience, since it deals with a critical phase of Australian history, in the early days of the Second World War. But it is also a manuscript which has for years been 'raided' by writers in search of juicy quotations, often taken out of context, to support particular views of Menzies. It is therefore important that the Diary should be available in its original and total form, so that readers might be in a position fully to assess the glosses which have been put upon it. It is also important that we attempt from the outset to avoid an anachronistic approach and recognise the Diary for what it is: a historical document created at a particular time and in a particular place, to be appreciated in its own context and not according to the values of a later period.

The Diary is contained in three ruled exercise books with plain black covers, labelled 'A', 'B' and 'C'. The daily entries are in flowing handwriting, in pencil, with scarcely a sign of correction or hesitation throughout. Menzies exhausted space in one exercise book before moving to its successor. Since the division into three volumes in the original Diary is arbitrary and the entries are sequential, we have for the purposes of publication melded them together and reproduced the text in three logical sections. Linking passages (in italics) are intended broadly to explain to the reader how these sections fit together, while showing briefly the sequence of experiences recorded in each.

The transcription of the Diary is as far as possible an exact replication of the original, reproducing all punctuation, underlining, abbreviations, capitalisations, etc., as in Menzies' original handwriting. Our only insertions in the Diary (apart from footnote reference numbers) are the linking passages mentioned above and notes to indicate where Menzies began another exercise book. Parentheses and the information inserted within are Menzies' additions, not the editors'. Obvious errors and omissions are not corrected, although apart from occasional misspelling of place names and proper names mistakes are very rare. Fortunately, too, the handwriting is generally clear and easy to decipher. Only towards the end of the trip, during his hurried visit to the United States, does the clarity falter. Here the entries deteriorate into notes, hastily written and sometimes difficult to read with confidence.

We use footnotes to identify important individuals, giving as far as possible the rank or position each person occupied at the time of Menzies' visit and, where necessary, to correct his spelling of names, as well as to provide other useful information. To avoid excessive cluttering of the pages, however, we do not identify more obscure individuals whom Menzies transiently meets, nor do we explain every passing reference. The Diary, as a day-to-day record of events, is naturally not always self-explanatory so we have added appendixes to clarify for the general reader some key issues which need to be understood, and which involve other sources to supplement the Diary. We have also had free access to, and permission to publish items from, the Menzies Family Papers through the courtesy of Heather (Mrs Peter Henderson), the daughter of Sir Robert Menzies.

INTRODUCTION

Robert Gordon Menzies was not normally a diarist. A busy barrister and a highly active politician, he preferred to use any spare time he had on other things: family, reading, good fellowship in clubs like the Savage, following the art of cricket and musing on it. Neither of the factors which seem most to animate avid diarists, the urge for self-analysis and the love of gossip, particularly interested him. But on two occasions, when he made trips abroad, he did keep a quite detailed account of his experiences and the sentiments they evoked. The first was in 1935 when, accompanied by his wife Pat, Menzies made his first trip to England. This diary begins on 19 February 1935, the day on which the couple sailed out of Port Phillip Bay and ends on 8 September, the day on which they arrived back. It was a great adventure, made in the days when even for a minister of the Crown (Menzies was then federal Attorney-General) the opportunity for international travel was rare. In this case the trip took on additional excitement from the fact that Menzies was one of a ministerial party visiting London for trade talks and the celebration of George V's Silver Jubilee. In the circumstances, Pat, thinking that the Menzies children would in due course value a careful record of what their parents had seen and done, insisted that her husband keep a diary, and stood over him each day to make sure he made an entry.[1] In so doing she also unwittingly won for posterity an engaging record of how it was that her husband's reverence for things British took new shape and substance as he abandoned himself—as he put it—'to those reflections which can so strangely (unless you remember our traditions and upbringing) move the souls of those who go "home" to a land they have never seen'.[2]

The second diary is the one published here, recording a wartime trip Menzies made to England as Prime Minister of Australia in 1941. Again it begins on the day he left, 24 January, and ends on 24 May, the eve of his arrival home. This time his wife had necessarily to remain in Australia but the incentive to keep a diary was strong, even without the discipline she might have imposed. The sense of being involved behind the scenes as well as before the public in history-making events was enough to make Menzies take up his pen every day, just as it sustained his busyness with the cine-camera that had become the instrument of an almost obsessive hobby.

---

1   Menzies explains this in the preface to 'Jubilee Pilgrim', an unpublished book he wrote in 1936 from his 1935 Diary.

2   Menzies 1935 Diary, 21 March.

Menzies had made two other trips to England and Europe between 1935 and 1941; one in 1936 (alone) and the other in 1938 (again accompanied by his wife). That he kept diaries on neither does not betoken laziness or a sense that what he was seeing and experiencing was insignificant. He wrote home to his family long personal letters of which, fortunately, many have been preserved. Chiefly as far as his social life and his pleasure at being in England are concerned, they are a valuable substitute for diaries, though they lack the continuity, the sense of wholeness, that diaries give.

Wholeness and immediacy: these are the qualities that make Menzies' 1941 Diary so valuable a document. It is a spontaneous day-to-day record of events as they took place, seen through the eyes of a notably intelligent man, who as a trained barrister and experienced politician was used to making firm and frank judgements on men and events. What he writes of course tells us as much about Menzies himself as about those whom he describes and evaluates: about the outlook which his time, his social background and his professional training had ingrained, not to speak of his own personality. And since the writing is so spontaneous—indeed artless—moods vary and attitudes to people and issues can be ambivalent. But what above all gives the Diary its life and authority is its record of Menzies' feelings about events *as they happened*. And on another level, the detailed record of his activities registers just how busy he was, pursuing the purposes that had brought him to England and following through on unexpected activities and responsibilities in which he became implicated while he was there. This was far from being the ineffectual trip that Menzies' detractors, then and since, have often claimed it to have been. Many years after its creation, when as an old man he sat down to write his memoir *Afternoon Light*, Menzies opened the Diary, registered pain at what he found there, and loftily mused on the rarity of diarists like Pepys, Evelyn and Greville. In the case of ordinary mortals, he wrote, a private diary was unlikely to be 'a great source of entertainment': its main human usefulness was to be 'a reminder of past error'. For

> I cannot read this limited 1941 diary of my own without blushing for my readiness to make snap judgements and to resort to easy epigram ... I was, of course, many years younger than I am now, and consequently more prone to intolerance and hasty judgements. 'My salad days, When I was green in judgment.' My executors will do me a good service if they use the incinerator freely.[3]

---

3   Robert G. Menzies, *Afternoon Light: Some Memories of Men and Events* (Melbourne, 1967), pp. 44–5.

That Menzies left it to his executors to use the incinerator rather than doing so himself suggests that, despite his self-deprecatory remarks, he had a sneaking understanding that the Diary was a historical document of considerable significance. He used it as the chief warrant for the chapter—'Two Crucial Years: 1939–41'— which in *Afternoon Light* caught with some success the atmosphere of the wartime England he visited. The 'snap judgements' he deplored were criticisms, sometimes devastating, of a number of British politicians—Clement Attlee, Ernest Bevin, 'Bobbety' Salisbury (then Cranborne), Oliver Lyttelton and, above all, Winston Churchill—all of whom, he says, he came later to respect and admire.[4] A quarter of a century separated the events recorded in the Diary from the writing of *Afternoon Light*, whose interpretations could not but be affected by what had come between, especially during Menzies' long, and ultimately somewhat complacent, second period as Australia's Prime Minister from 1949 to 1966. The tensions of wartime Imperial relations had by then faded, and though he could still speak sharply about the need for greater consultation within the British Commonwealth Menzies, on his now frequent trips to England, met and dealt with politicians and civil servants in a mostly relaxed and often purely ceremonial atmosphere. With Churchill in particular he established a comfortable friendship. As time passed, the two men thought of themselves as elder statesmen of an Empire whose changing character they mutually deplored. Decolonisation and the admission to Commonwealth counsels of leaders of hitherto subject peoples were not to their taste, and they found it hard to think of republics as members of the British family in quite the same way as the old white Dominions had been. Looking back on the Allies' ultimate victory over Hitler and Mussolini, it was easy for Menzies to play down Churchill's foibles and idolise him as the great leader and saviour of his country. So at Churchill's funeral he could provide a noble tribute and in *Afternoon Light* he gave on him a 'last will and testament'. To all who would know Churchill only through the pages of books, some of them critical, Menzies had one simple thing to say: 'you have not lived on the barricades of a great war, or been sustained and brought to victory by the greatest man of the century.'[5]

That mellow judgement, however, does nothing to expunge the curious love-hate relationship which in reality developed during Menzies' first sustained encounter with Churchill. The two men had met briefly in 1935 when Maurice Hankey, the celebrated Cabinet Secretary and British *éminence grise* who had visited Melbourne in the previous year and become a friend, took Menzies to visit Churchill at his estate, Chartwell. They found their quarry wallowing in a

---

4 Ibid., pp. 45 and 62–94.

5 Ibid., p. 94; and see Appendix III 'Appraising Churchill'.

swimming pool he had constructed with his own hands and subsequently at tea listened to him working himself up on the subject of the parlous state of the nation's defences. 'My impression,' wrote Menzies, 'is of a man who lives too well and lacks that philosophical mental self-discipline which prevents a man from going to excesses either of mind or body. But an arresting person—and I had no delusions of grandeur in his presence!'[6] His reaction was rather more sour a few weeks later when in the House of Commons he sat in the gallery and heard Churchill speak in the debate on the Stresa agreement, which announced the first Franco-British determination to resist Hitler's claims against the Versailles Treaties. 'The idol,' wrote Menzies, 'has feet of clay.' Churchill *read* his speech, thus breaking Menzies' primary test of what constituted a good public speaker; more serious, 'his theme is a constant repetition of "I told you so", and a first class man usually doesn't indulge in this luxury. If a first-rater has once said an important thing, he doesn't need to remind people that he's said it.'[7] When Menzies set out for England in 1941 Churchill's position in British politics had of course changed fundamentally. From being in 1935 a seemingly eccentric voice crying in the wilderness against British supineness and reluctance to resist the European dictators, he had become by 1941 the wartime Prime Minister of a nation fighting for its very existence. But Menzies still had reservations, at least about Churchill's style, before they met again. On 9 February 1941, while in Egypt *en route* to England, he listened, with British military chiefs, as

> Winston Churchill broadcasts, to the pleasure of all save myself. No doubt Winston is right to appeal to the lowest common denominator among men—a hymn of hate—"the black hearted, treacherous Italians" &c, but I am quite sure we have a loftier cause than the one his speeches indicate.[8]

This was a mood which hardly seemed to bode well for good relations in the days that lay ahead.

Though of central importance, Menzies' personal encounter with Churchill was of course not his only preoccupation during the visit to England in 1941. This was a period of great anxiety, when Australian military forces, in North Africa and the Mediterranean area, were for the first time engaged in the Second World War, at first in victories which Menzies rejoiced in, but then in

---

6   Menzies 1935 Diary, 25 and 26 May.

7   Menzies 1935 Diary, 2 May.

8   Menzies 1941 Diary, 9 February.

suffering which resulted, as he saw it, from British decisions he was powerless to alter. Moreover, with war threatening in the Pacific, Menzies had come to England primarily to protest at the parlous state of British defences at Singapore and to discuss matters of trade and the production of munitions and aircraft. He and his two advisers, Frederick Shedden, head of Defence Co-ordination, and John Storey of the Aircraft Production Commission (two secretaries, Norman C. Tritton and Samuel Landau, completed the small Australian party) carried out a taxing schedule of talks on these issues with British ministers, civil servants and industrialists. Many of Menzies' hours and much of his nervous energy went into his regular attendance at meetings of the British War Cabinet, to which Churchill from the outset invited him. At the same time, he came to know at first hand the German bombing 'blitz' on London and other English cities. Overwhelmed by the British civilian population's courage in the face of an ordeal hitherto beyond his imagining, he took every opportunity to speak public words of praise and comfort. For audiences ranging from literati in bookshops to factory workers in the Midlands he offered the reassurance that they were not fighting alone, that Australia, though at the other end of the earth, had sent troops and munitions to help, and that her admiration for what the British were doing was boundless. Menzies' fine oratorical skills were never better displayed than in these addresses and he was often rapturously received. So much so, indeed, that after one particularly moving experience of this kind he spontaneously confided to his Diary: 'Impression grows that best value of this mission is to encourage and lift up the people here. They have had a bad time and want a boost to their spirits.'[9] At the behest of the publishers Longmans Green and Co. he polished for publication the text of sixteen of these hortatory speeches, and the slender volume which resulted, *To the People of Britain at War*, appeared before the end of 1941.

Menzies was taken by surprise at the bitter feelings he discovered, from the very day of his arrival in London, against southern Ireland's insistence, under the steely grip of Eamon de Valera, the Prime Minister of Eire, on maintaining its neutrality in the war. He did not know, until he sat in the War Cabinet and learnt details of horrific shipping losses (which, with wartime censorship, could never be revealed publicly), how close Britain was coming to strangulation through the depredations on her Atlantic lifeline of German U-boat packs and heavy bombers. The enemy was immeasurably aided by the inability of British air and sea forces to use as bases the so-called 'Treaty Ports' which had once been at their disposal in Ireland but which had been ceded to independent Eire as recently as 1938 by Neville Chamberlain's 'appeasing'

---

9   Menzies 1941 Diary, 26 February.

Government. Knowing that the survival of Britain was crucial for the Empire as a whole, Menzies conceived the quixotic hope that as an important outsider he might have some influence with de Valera. Against the explicit wish of Churchill, whose hatred for the Irish leader was deep and venomous, Menzies therefore visited Ireland, spent a day conferring with de Valera and wrote a long and impassioned report recommending meaningful negotiations between London and Dublin. Predictably enough, Churchill almost contemptuously rejected Menzies' suggestions, and this was undoubtedly an important element in their deteriorating relations in the later stages of the Australian Prime Minister's visit.[10]

All the same there were of course some pleasant social diversions, not least of them—even despite developing tensions—weekends spent at Chequers, the British Prime Minister's country retreat. Here, almost to the end, Menzies was welcome, in Churchill's words, as a man 'with whom it is agreeable to dine'.[11] There were always interesting fellow-guests to meet at Chequers and from his previous visits to England Menzies had a wide circle of personal friends although, as he observed gloomily at one point, these were

> dark and hurrying days in London, where the old pleasure of being here has gone, your old friends, all busy, are ships that pass in the night, a new spectacle of ruin meets you at every turn, the air raid warning wails every night, and the only comfort is that the purple crocuses are out in the park opposite.[12]

And always in the background was his insecure political position at home. His parliamentary majority was tenuous, and he suffered constant press and Opposition attacks for supposed failure to stand up for Australian interests in Britain; attacks whose injustice he could never fully contest because of the confidentiality of the War Cabinet and ministerial discussions in which he was involved. Alarming messages, chiefly from his wife, warned of plots against his leadership, within his own and the Country parties. Although in constant cable communication with his Cabinet and his Acting Prime Minister, Arthur Fadden, it was always difficult for Menzies to convey the inwardness of his conversations and activities in London, and there is often an unfair note of peevishness in the telegrams he received from his colleagues in Australia. In the face of the ominous situation which developed for

---

10   See Appendix II 'The Trip to Ireland'.

11   John Colville, *Footprints in Time* (London, 1976), p. 129.

12   Menzies 1941 Diary, 10 March.

Australian soldiers in Greece during the last weeks of his stay Menzies twice delayed his return to Australia because, as he wrote in his Diary, grave decisions had to be made about troop movements, 'and I am not content to have them solved by "unilateral rhetoric"'.[13] The jibe at Churchill was repeated confidentially to Fadden, but it could not be generally known even to Menzies' wife.

The Diary offers a rich elaboration of these and many other matters. But it needs first to be placed in its Australian context by observing the political circumstances in which Menzies undertook the trip and what the motives were that prompted it.

Menzies became Prime Minister of Australia late in April 1939, by virtue of his election to the leadership of the United Australia Party (UAP), replacing Joseph Lyons. Lyons had died suddenly a few weeks before, at Easter. The UAP at that point had no deputy leader. Menzies, who had for some years been Lyons' Attorney-General and deputy, and who on various occasions had been led to believe that Lyons would pass the leadership on to him, resigned his office barely a month before Lyons' death. He did so in protest at a Government decision virtually to abandon a scheme for National Insurance, a cause to which he was deeply committed. Lyons headed a UAP–Country Party Coalition and on his death, there being no automatic UAP successor to him, the leader of the Country Party, Earle Page, became caretaker Prime Minister, until such time as the UAP could elect a successor to Lyons. Page made it clear that, once the election had taken place, he would make way, as was customary, for the leader of the senior party to become Prime Minister. But he also let it be known that if Menzies became the new leader he, Page, would not serve in a Menzies-led Ministry: in effect, that the Coalition would be at an end.

Page's antipathy towards Menzies had both a personal and a party basis. Temperamentally, the gap between the two men was immense. A country doctor and crafty politician, Page all the same lacked flair. He had initially encountered Menzies in 1934, when the latter came at the age of thirty-nine to federal politics and the Attorney-Generalship after brief but successful ministerial experience in Victoria. The new Attorney-General was a witty, intelligent barrister who from the first overshadowed Page, then Minister for Commerce. The personal contrast, exacerbated by Menzies' sometimes biting tongue and noteworthy

13   Menzies 1941 Diary, 14 April.

capacity for acid mimicry, was seconded by a party contrast. From his Victorian experience Menzies brought to the federal sphere a suspicion of, shading into contempt for, the Country Party as a narrow and sectional pressure group not attuned to the lofty notions of public service which he laid claim to. Conflict in 1938–39 over National Insurance, which the Country Party sabotaged but which Menzies and UAP colleagues like Richard Casey warmly supported, deepened the rift on party grounds. But it seems that the most profound personal antagonism arose from serious friction between Page and Menzies when they were in London as Australian ministers in 1936 and 1938 to negotiate trade agreements with the British. After coming home Menzies talked 'in terms', as one contemporary reported, 'so contemptuous of Page that I have gasped; and of course, these strictures have got back to Page, and he has brooded over them so long that when his resentment did find expression, it, too, was something that took one's breath away'.[14]

Page made a scabrous attack on Menzies when announcing in Parliament that he was resigning the Acting Prime Ministership and would not serve in a Menzies Government. Menzies, he said, could not provide the leadership desperately needed by a country facing the prospect of war: not only had he proved disloyal to his erstwhile leader, Lyons, but unless he could publicly explain his failure to enlist in the First World War he would not command the maximum effort of the Australian people in the event of another war. Distress at Lyons' death, which Page, as medical adviser and close friend, felt keenly, partly excuses this extraordinary attack, but it remained that the charge of disloyalty was unproven and that the question of enlistment, as Menzies said in a dignified reply, was one that relates 'to a man's intimate, personal and family affairs' and for which no answer can 'be made on the public platform'.[15] Though the incident caused him pain it probably in the end benefited Menzies: Stanley Melbourne Bruce, the Australian High Commissioner in London, was not far off the mark when he wrote ironically: 'There is no doubt that Page was your fairy godfather, if you had the slightest desire to be Prime Minister. Apparently he had considerable objection to your being one and promptly took the only possible course which would make the job a sitting certainty for you.'[16] But though Page's extraordinary assault generated much sympathy for Menzies, it remained that others shared resentment against Menzies' often arrogant ways. His election to the leadership was perhaps, given his intellectual superiority over other

---

14   The journalist and *Times* correspondent, R.L. Curthoys. See A.W. Martin, *Robert Menzies: A Life, vol. 1, 1894–1943* (Melbourne, 1993), p. 278.

15   Commonwealth of Australia, *Parliamentary Debates*, 19 April 1939 to June 1939, vol. 159, p. 19.

16   Bruce to Menzies, 4 October 1939, Menzies Family Papers.

contenders, inevitable; but it was far from unanimous. Menzies had never deigned to cultivate popularity in the party. There were some who were jealous of his gifts and found his obvious ambition distasteful; others had been offended by his sharp tongue and superior ways which gave too ready an impression of arrogance.

Moreover, the political balance was from Menzies' point of view scarcely propitious when he came to power. His party, the UAP, had emerged in 1931 from the cauldron of the Great Depression as a party of 'sanity' and orthodoxy. Menzies had been one of those who behind the scenes canalised into the new political formation a largely spontaneous explosion of predominantly middle class organisations like the All for Australia League, which demanded 'honest' solutions to economic ills. He had also played a major part in persuading Labor's erstwhile Treasurer, Joseph Lyons, to become the leader of the UAP. James Scullin's Labor Government, split disastrously by the agonising issues raised by the Depression, was no match for the new party. Lyons' simplicity and patent honesty were furthermore winning electoral qualities, and in 1931 and 1934 the UAP–Country Party Coalition swept the polls. But then, when the economic situation began to improve, it became a question whether the UAP, formed to cope with an emergency, could find effective principles to hold itself together. By 1937, when the next federal election fell due, the party—and the Government— seemed divided and faltering, held together mainly by the conciliatory leadership of Lyons, whose health was however becoming more and more fragile. On the other side, Labor was regaining strength and unity under its new leader, John Curtin. Whether the Government could win a third term of office (a feat not hitherto achieved by any combination since the coming of Federation) was a serious question: though Lyons had wanted to hand over the leadership to Menzies in 1936, the party managers prevailed on him to stay on, as a sure election winner, for the 1937 contest. And his presence as leader is, indeed, generally taken to account for the unexpected outcome of that election: a new House of Representatives in which the balance of parties was little changed.

The situation was very different at the next election, held in September 1940. Lyons' magic was no longer there and Menzies, at the head of a divided party, was Prime Minister of a country now at war. Though Australian soldiers, sailors and airmen were already deployed to fight overseas, the war still seemed remote to many at home. Hence in seeking to put the nation on an effective war footing Menzies and his ministers struggled against widespread apathy. On the other hand there were also those, especially in the press, who became carping critics of a supposed sluggishness in the Government's war effort. And shortly before the election, Menzies suffered a terrible personal and political blow when three of his staunchest ministers and supporters, Geoffrey Street, James Fairbairn and Henry Gullett, were killed in a plane crash near Canberra. In the election, Menzies asked the voters to be decisive: to give his Government sound endorsement or clear defeat. In the upshot he received neither. The UAP–Country Party Coalition and the Australian Labor Party (ALP) won an equal number of seats, and two Independent members held the balance of power. The Government's most serious losses were in New South Wales where the *Sydney Morning Herald* and the *Daily Telegraph* had damned it with faint praise and demanded new blood in Parliament and Ministry. Difficult, perhaps unstable, government had now to be faced at what was a critical phase in the nation's history. Menzies proposed as a solution the formation of a national, all-party government, but a special ALP interstate conference had before the election ruled this possibility out. Curtin suggested as an alternative a purely Advisory War Council, on which Government and Opposition would have equal representation, and which the Government could inform and consult on all matters to do with the conduct of the war. Menzies reluctantly agreed: an Opposition which received classified information, gave appropriately informed advice and yet took no responsibility for any decisions that followed was not to his taste. But he announced that he and his colleagues were determined to try to achieve effective cooperation with the Opposition in the months ahead.

It was against this shaky political background that plans for Menzies to make a brief visit to England took shape. Late in October 1940 as a result of an earlier suggestion by the British Chiefs of Staff, Australian and New Zealand officers met with British officers in Singapore to discuss Far Eastern defence; a matter becoming increasingly urgent in the light of Japan's menacing southward movement to Indo-China. The conference agreed that Malaya's security was the key to the safety of Australia and New Zealand, but spelt out grave deficiencies, in military and air strength as well as in naval force, in Singapore's defences.[17] British neglect of this situation was by now a running sore and, in particular, Churchill's penchant for playing down the danger to Singapore was notorious. In 1939, for example, when he was First Lord of the Admiralty, he had in an appreciation of the Far Eastern situation pooh-poohed the idea of Singapore ever succumbing to land-based attack: 'it could only be taken after a siege by an army of at least 50,000 men, who would have to be landed in the marshes and jungles of the Isthmus which connects it to the mainland.' Such a siege would last four to five months at least, which would give Great Britain plenty of time to send a superior naval force to the scene.[18] The detailed findings of the Singapore Conference of 1940 underlined the hollowness of such a view, and after he read these findings Menzies wired to Cranborne, the Dominions Minister, his

---

17   Hasluck, pp. 295–6.

18   Paper of 17 November 1939 for a meeting of Dominion Ministers on the Naval Defence of Australia, PRO CAB 99/1/141.

Government's strong feeling that personal contact between Empire countries was essential in the near future 'if Empire military plans [were] to be concerted and our common strategic ideas to be brought up to date'. He instanced Australia's special interests in the Middle East (where Australian troops now were), Singapore and the western Pacific and declared that 'as Prime Minister I would be willing to go to London or any other nominated place to attend the necessary conference'.[19] Nothing came of this proposal, so a few weeks later the Advisory War Council discussed at Menzies' instigation 'the alarming position' revealed at the Singapore Conference. The Prime Minister intimated his wish to go personally to discuss this and other matters with Churchill, and secured the council's agreement that he should do so.[20] By so agreeing, the Labor members of the council implicitly (though not formally) gave the Government immunity during Menzies' absence: without this, he could not have gone. On 1 December the Commonwealth Government sent a long cable to Cranborne expressing its grave concern at the 'most serious position' revealed by the report of the Singapore Conference and offering to help with equipment, ammunition and a brigade of the Australian Imperial Force (AIF) to operate temporarily in Malaya until they could be relieved by Indian troops—but stressing the urgent need for aircraft and naval reinforcements from Britain.[21] Just before Christmas Cranborne replied that 'Eastern anxieties' must be borne 'patiently and doggedly' until Italy was 'broken as a combatant'. In the Mediterranean and in the Atlantic

> we are at the fullest naval strain I have seen either in this or former war. The only way in which a naval squadron could be found for Singapore would be by ruining the Mediterranean situation. This, I am sure, you would not wish us to do unless or until the Japanese danger becomes far more menacing than at present. I am also persuaded that if Japan should enter into the war, the United States will come in on our side, which will put the naval boot very much on the other leg.[22]

A few days before this rather depressing message arrived, Menzies wired Bruce to say that Parliament had just adjourned until March 1941, and that he thought of leaving in January for a quick trip to England 'to discuss matters of mutual war importance', visiting Australian troops in the Middle East on the way. Could Bruce confirm that this would be agreeable to the British

---

19   Menzies to Cranborne, 8 November 1940, *DAFP*, vol. IV, p. 263.

20   Advisory War Council Minute, 25 November 1940, *DAFP*, vol. IV, pp. 282–3.

21   Commonwealth Government to Cranborne, 1 December 1940, *DAFP*, vol. IV, pp. 285–7.

22   Cranborne to Commonwealth Government, 23 December 1940, *DAFP*, vol. IV, p. 315.

Government?[23] Bruce spoke to Churchill who asked him to tell Menzies 'how greatly your visit will be welcomed and how much he personally would appreciate your presence here'.[24] But by the beginning of January Menzies briefly appeared to have second thoughts, perhaps put off a little by Cranborne's discouraging message of 23 December, perhaps influenced by his wife, who was strongly opposed to his making the trip. Pat Menzies was well aware both of dissidence within her husband's own following and of the anxiety of a section of the Labor Party, led by the newly-elected H.V. Evatt, to overthrow him, and thought it crucial that he stay and guard his own position.[25] On 3 January Menzies told Bruce that he was 'a good deal exercised' about whether it was wise to go, 'as political position here precarious and principal lieutenants in Cabinet not very experienced'. But, on the other hand, he felt that 'much mutual benefit might result from visit provided I could be sure of prompt and sufficient opportunity for consultation with Churchill and chief Ministers'. In particular, he felt that if he could get some clear picture of 'where we stand in the Far East and reasonably long range policy of Middle East' he would be in a better position to plan the deployment of Australia's manpower more soundly. He was also interested 'to give United Kingdom Government a clear picture of amazing munitions potential developed and developing here and to see how far greater joint use could be arranged'. What would Bruce's frank advice be about what he should do?[26]

Bruce's reply, a long and plain-spoken cable, pointed out that in making his decision Menzies must weigh the political position in Australia (on which, at his distance he, Bruce, could offer 'little useful comment') against the possible results he could achieve in London. On that he had some disconcerting things to say:

> Prompt and sufficient opportunity for consultation with Chief Ministers would be forthcoming but this of limited value. As regards major policy as this increasingly centred in Prime Minister's hands and little influenced by other members of War Cabinet who frankly are not prepared to stand up to him, my view is Prime Minister would endeavour treat you in much same way—most cordial welcome—utmost courtesy—invitation to attend meetings of War Cabinet and apparently every possible opportunity for consultation. When however you tried to pin him down to definite discussions of fundamental questions of major war policy I am inclined to think you would find him discursive and elusive necessitating your either (a) taking a line that would mean a considerable show down between you or (b) leaving with a sense of frustration.

23   Menzies to Bruce, 17 December 1940, *DAFP*, vol. IV, p. 303.
24   Bruce to Menzies, 18 December 1940, *DAFP*, vol. IV, p. 308.
25   Interview with Dame Pattie Menzies, 1 October 1987.
26   Menzies to Bruce, 3 January 1941, *DAFP*, vol. IV, p. 320.

In England at the moment, Bruce added, 'everything is governed by what Hitler's next move is going to be—it is difficult to see how it can be other than on the grand scale'. He meant that everyone was now waiting to see whether the German air offensive on the British Isles was the prelude to invasion and he made it clear that, until that danger was over, other matters of major policy were unlikely to receive very serious attention. 'While I would greatly desire your visit and feel strongly you would do most valuable service in your discussions with Ministers here,' Bruce concluded, 'I have given you the points I feel you must take into account in making your decision.'[27] If these considerations gave Menzies further pause it was not for long. Preparations for the trip continued, and on 24 January, in the manner noted in the first entry of the Diary, it began. Menzies, supported by both his War Cabinet and the Advisory War Council, kept to his determination to press the British on Singapore and to negotiate agreement on further development of wartime industry in Australia. No doubt for him personally there was the added, if not to be trumpeted, pleasure he always had in travel to his beloved England, in this case spiced by the extra thrill of danger due to the war. Nor could Menzies be unaware that this was a particularly apt time to be representing Australia in London. In this dark hour of Hitler's threat to the homeland itself, the one ray of light in a gloomy war situation had been recent achievements of Australian arms in the Middle East. Australia's name was consequently an honoured one and as Australia's Prime Minister Menzies felt he would be welcomed and listened to. Besides, he glowed at the thought of visiting his troops on the way to England.

The particular troops in question were the men of the 6th Division of the AIF, the war's first Australian volunteers for military service abroad. In the First World War, the original AIF had been organised in five divisions: recruiting the initial soldiers of a second AIF into a sixth division was a way of emphasising a continuing tradition. The first drafts of this division went into camp in October 1939, after the Canadians had promised a contingent for Europe by December, and the British were anxious to see by the same date equivalent Australian and New Zealand forces for what the Secretary of State for War, Anthony Eden, believed to be the salutary 'psychological effect on our French friends and on Germany of the knowledge that these troops will be in the field in France, probably in time for a spring campaign'.[28] Menzies was opposed to sending Australian troops away until security in the Pacific was properly provided for: 'this is not 1914,' he told his critics, 'when there was no real problem of Australia's security from attack, and when land forces in Europe were the

---

27   Bruce to Menzies, 5 January 1941, *DAFP*, vol. IV, pp. 325–6.

28   Eden to Chamberlain, 3 November 1939, *DAFP*, vol. II, p. 369.

determining factor.'[29] But British machinations and a unilateral announcement by the New Zealand Government that it would match the Canadian commitment forced his hand. The 6th Division embarked in February 1940 for Egypt where, following the precedent set in the previous war, it was to complete its training for action in Europe.

But within months the fall of France and the simultaneous entry of Italy into the war abruptly altered this strategic picture. Instead of helping to mount the expected spring campaign on the Continent, Britain found herself fighting alone, enduring air attack and bracing herself for an expected German invasion. For the moment, no substantial reinforcements could be spared for other theatres, of which, as it happened, the most vital was North Africa. There the Italians had upwards of half a million troops, deployed in their colony, Libya, and their lately taken Abyssinian territories. This army could only be a standing menace to the British position in Egypt, and especially to the Suez Canal. The British forces then on the ground and at the disposal of the Commander-in-Chief, General Sir Archibald Wavell, seemed meagre indeed: the British 7th Armoured Division, the not fully trained and equipped Australian 6th Division, and the Indian 5th Division. But in an extraordinarily short campaign, these troops routed the Italians and won the first major Allied land victory since the outbreak of the war.

Wavell opened this operation at the end of 1940, driving away from Suez into Libya. The Indians took Sidi Barrani then were sent to Abyssinia, and the British armour and Australian infantry carried out the rest of the Libyan campaign. In a rapid sweep forward, the Australians captured the major Italian position of Bardia (3 January) and the port of Tobruk (22 January). Two weeks later, on 7 February, they took the stronghold of Benghazi, having advanced 500 miles in a little over a month. The Italians, poorly led, and with weapons that were often obsolete, failed to acquit themselves well. Great numbers were taken prisoner and immense quantities of equipment were captured or destroyed. Menzies' excitement at the prospect of visiting the victorious Australian troops was understandable. As he flew out of Australia on 24 January, the great news was of the capture of Tobruk. Before he reached the Middle East, Benghazi had fallen. For any Australian Prime Minister these would have been heady days.

---

29   *Age*, 26 September 1939.

THE DIARY

24 January – 24 May 1941

24 January – 19 February

Menzies leaves Rose Bay, Sydney, by flying boat on 24 January. An anxious wife, with his father-in-law, Senator John Leckie, and others of his ministerial colleagues see him off. He reaches Darwin on 26 January, then travels to Singapore via the Netherlands East Indies. Talks with government and military leaders in the latter two places confirm his conviction of the need for stepped up security against the threat of Japanese aggression. Heading for the Middle East he visits the Thai Prime Minister in Bangkok, is received by British officials on a steam launch on the Irrawaddy, marvels at the Indian countryside and revels in 'cool and civilised' entertainment at Karachi. In Baluchistan he is greeted by a guard of honour 'who present arms with great snap', and in the Shatt-al-Arab Hotel at Basra he enjoys partridge, foie gras, chablis and Nuits St George. Flying westward across the Tigris-Euphrates delta he sees Baghdad, marvels at patches of cultivation in mountainous Trans-Jordan and suddenly sees below, the Sea of Galilee and the 'lone green wonder of the Jordan valley'.

Landing at Tiberias on 2 February, Menzies is met by Lieutenant-General Blamey, Commander of the AIF troops in the Middle East, and Sir Harold MacMichael, British High Commissioner in Palestine. He quickly revels, as a good Presbyterian, in Jerusalem and the biblical scenes he can identify. But there is stern contemporary relevance in the official duties which at once occupy him: inspection of a military hospital, drinks at an officers mess, and a march past of AIF troops whom he afterwards addresses through amplifiers. A busy run of days follow. With Cairo as his base, Menzies inspects Australian warships serving with the British Mediterranean fleet, visits troops at Bardia and Tobruk, and flies in pursuit of the victorious 6th Division units which have just taken Benghazi. There he addresses his Australian soldiers and their officers, experiences his first air raid, and is indignant about a British general who denounces to him the 'irregular' conduct of Australians on guard duty but says 'nothing about their great fighting'. Cairo, as administrative centre and military headquarters, also involves tiring diplomatic and social responsibilities. At the end, on 13 February: 'I have worked like a nigger for these 10 days, but I think the results may be of great value.'

Resuming his journey, Menzies visits Khartoum, Lagos and Lisbon before at last landing in England. His long trip, which ends on the south coast, at Poole, has taken a few days short of a month.

16

Australia—Egypt—London—Ottawa—Washington
1941

Friday – Jan 24th 1941

Leave Sydney.[1] Qantas Empire Flying Boat CORINNA Capt R.S. Adair. The aircraft so streamlined that looked at from the rear it looks positively herring-gutted, but from inside it is most roomy—comfortable seats in which you may snooze not only post-prandially but all day.

(Sydney to Brisbane 480 miles, Brisbane to Gladstone 280 miles)

Fadden,[2] Collins,[3] McBride,[4] John Leckie[5] come to see us off. Glad J.L. there, because whole business is distressing to Pat who has vast courage but knows that for once in my life I am off upon a chancy undertaking.[6]

Chief feature in the air—press the button and the steward arrives with the drinks—the Company's compliments in our case. Shedden and I, each of whom had dived into his pockets for cash, smile with genuine Scottish pleasure.

At Brisbane, a few moments with Sir Fergus McMaster (one of my New Year Knights). He is concerned with war-time penetration by Pan American not only via Auckland, but via Singapore, which would be fatal to Qantas. Conferred Hudson Fysh (who was at Rose Bay at our departure) regarding importance of Dilli. [Should cable Fadden about this].[7]

Have our first adventure after leaving Gladstone—a hot and dismal looking place with a meat works. Strong head winds (monsoon weather) grew into a gale of hurricane force—at least 60 m.p.h., and, about opposite Mackay the Capt. decided to return to Gladstone, fearing a dark arrival and petrol shortage. A hot night in Gladstone where "received by the Mayor" informally at

---

1   Menzies' party consisted of Frederick G. Shedden, head of Defence Co-ordination; John Storey of the Aircraft Production Commission; and two secretaries, Norman C. Tritton and Samuel Landau.

2   Arthur Fadden, leader of the Country Party and Deputy Prime Minister, was Acting Prime Minister while Menzies was overseas.

3   Thomas Joseph Collins, Honorary Minister.

4   Senator Philip Albert Martin McBride, Minister for Supply and Development, and always one of Menzies' staunchest supporters.

5   Senator John William Leckie, Honorary Minister and Menzies' father-in-law.

6   'Pat' is Menzies' wife.

7   Sir Fergus McMaster, grazier and businessman, had, along with P.J. McGinness and Hudson Fysh, founded Qantas airlines in 1920. In 1938 Qantas had opened its England–Australia flying boat service, on which the Prime Minister and his entourage were now travelling along with other commercial passengers. Concerned about the security of the Darwin–Dili service, Hudson Fysh, Managing Director of Qantas Empire Airways Limited, had visited Dili in January 1941 and advised the Australian Government on a proposal to station an officer of the Civil Aviation Department in Portuguese Timor to report on the local situation and to keep an eye on Japanese activities.

hotel and discover anew the great truth that Federal grants through States for purposes outside direct C'wealth responsibility are dubious. The C'wealth, pre-war, made a grant in aid of civil aerodromes. Other Queensland towns got some—Gladstone none. Result—sad memories and bitter injustice!!

Flying height—7500 ft–600 ft!!

Saturday Jan 25th

Gladstone to Townsville 440 miles. We shall lose a day over yesterday's turn back.

Surprised to see how much of this Queensland coast is rotten and swampy—mangrove swamps with big rivers running through them for as many miles as the eye can see.

Pass over famous Mackay harbour—purely artificial—in Forgan Smith's electorate.[8] Gladstone has a perfect natural harbour, with 36' of water at the wharf, but pots of money were spent constructing an artificial harbour at Rockhampton, only a few miles away. Marvellous State!

At Townsville, meet Hogan, Fadden's partner,[9] who has the interesting story to tell of a client with £7000 p.a. whose combined tax on the last £1000 is £1040! Must tell Frank Forde this. "Socking the rich"!![10]

Interesting talk at night with Shedden & Storey. Latter, shrewd and experienced in industry, makes strong point that Arbitration Court judges have done much harm by regarding "premium payments" over & above basic wage or prescribed minimum wage as some justification for increasing the basic rate; on the argument that "The employers have shown they agree men ought to be paid more." What a pity our wage-control system (pace Higgins J.) has all along tended to depress the relative pay of the skilled man and so helped to create a scarcity which is one of our gravest war-time problems.[11]

Sunday Jan 26th

Last night was a swelterer at Townsville, the worst I have struck. Slept about 4 hours; and the bed wet through in all material places. We did a smart

---

8   William Forgan Smith, Labor member for Mackay since 1915, had been Premier of Queensland since 1932 and was noted for his lavish public works program.

9   A.W. Fadden, Hogan & Co. was the Townsville branch of Fadden's firm of Chartered Accountants.

10   Francis Michael Forde, teacher, engineer and Labor politician, had been Deputy Leader of the federal Labor Party since 1932. He had also been one of the Labor representatives on the Advisory War Council since 1940.

11   In 1907 the 'Harvester Judgment' of Justice Higgins, President of the Commonwealth Arbitration Court, established the Australian basic wage by defining in terms of the needs of a family the 'fair and reasonable' pay which a manufacturer must concede under 'new protection' legislation to receive the shelter of a tariff.

walk before bed to encourage the liver. If the liver is the source of sweat, it was certainly encouraged.

Domestic note. Silk shirts are hopeless for the tropics. They are wet through in 5 minutes, and flap greasily on you for the rest of the day. This morning I put on my short sleeved aertex cotton shirt—an immense improvement; don't need to wear a singlet.

Across the peninsula to Karumba, at the mouth of the Norman River. The country-side green and wet—a great rain has just fallen. Shores of Gulf of Carpentaria not well defined, but fade out into the sea by a series of swamps and marshes.

Flying at 7000 feet, the air became agreeably cool. Tritton, with a superb touch of virtuosity (he of course thinks, or says, that the Queensland climate is perfect!), puts on a pullover!

Slight head wind, and average speed slow; too slow. Townsville to Karumba 410 miles in 205 minutes—120 m.p.h. We shall be constantly late, and of course have already lost a day. Meals are eccentric. Day before yesterday we lunched at 4 pm precisely, the steward being no doubt a reader and admirer of W.J. Locke's "Septimus".[12]

Three interesting small boys (named North), avec mère, from near Simla in India. When our passage is smooth, they become vocal and active, their shrill but precise English voices most interesting. When a few bumps come along, they become quiet—just as I do! The eldest has collected my autograph and assures me, with grave courtesy, that it is "the next best I have, after Rudyard Kipling's!"

Groote Eylandt for us was a circular blue lagoon, surrounded by a low scrub, a 500 yard jetty, and an airways station. The mission station is 50 miles away. 18 men at the airways station—no hotel, no women, no politicians, in fact, complete Nirvana. Leaving Groote, many islands in every direction—Blue Mud Bay well named, the water a curious light greeny blue, very opaque. Had no idea this northern coast so tremendously indented and broken by islands. Black spot in distance alleged to be aborigine spearing fish, but otherwise no signs of life. All country seen today is amazingly well timbered and green, and on the sandy site of the Groote Eylandt Station sweet well water is obtained at 9 ft! As we move across towards Darwin, there are great patches of stony & dry country, but very quickly we are back to green country, fresh looking timber and numerous streams—the whole producing a no doubt fraudulent impression, since we are merely viewing the combined effect of summer heat and tropical rainfall.

---

12   *Septimus*, written by William John Locke in 1908, was a popular novel about an eccentric young Englishman who was a mathematician, inventor and visionary, greatly unpredictable in his behaviour.

Capt. Adair says we may see a herd or two of buffaloes, the children of a dozen or so imported many years ago. But we don't.

"Septimus", the steward, produces lunch at 3 p.m. (3.30 E.S.T.). God knows why, but Tritton is going to enquire.

8000 feet.

Darwin: Aubrey and Hilda Abbott.[13] A "cool" and spacious Government House, the only untoward incident being that a green and red frog disputed the bathroom with me. Went in evening to Vestey's (now a barracks) for a very good troop concert (2/25th battalion, Col. Withy). I was called on for "a few words" and got a first class reception, thank heaven. This AIF battalion a little worried about the possibility of indefinite stay at Darwin but, in shorts and shirts, the fittest looking crowd I've seen.

Darwin, on the whole, a pleasant surprise—quite luxuriant growth of trees and shrubs, several beaches, all new houses very comfortable looking, military buildings very good. Am assured on every side that if it were not for the unions Darwin would progress. But laziness and incompetence are evident about the wharf and railway terminal.

Meet Tom Schuurmann[14] (inward bound) at G.H. and have interesting talk about the anomalous position of the N.E.I.[15]

[NB arriving at Darwin, intercepted and escorted by 3 Hudsons and 5 Wirraways. Curious "bottling" action of aircraft flying at same level noted for the first time.[16]

Monday 27th Jan

At dawn, off across the Timor Sea—500 miles. Cool enough for a lusty breakfast at 9000 ft. Curious how accustomed one becomes to flying over vast stretches of land and water. Australia is behind and the great adventure has begun.

---

13   Charles Lydiard Aubrey Abbott, the Administrator of the Northern Territory, had been Country Party member for Gwydir in the House of Representatives, 1925–29 and 1931–37. When he resigned from Parliament in 1937 to take up his Northern Territory post a Labor candidate, William James Scully, won the seat; an event which registered a severe decline in the fortunes of Joseph Lyons' Coalition Government.

14   Tom Elink Schuurman, Netherlands Consul-General in Australia. Holland was occupied by the Germans but the establishment of a Dutch Government in exile, in England, meant that the colonial government in the Netherlands East Indies remained intact. After Menzies' visit, vagueness about mutual defence needs was removed by a meeting of British, Australian and Dutch service representatives which planned strategy in detail should war ensue in the Pacific. Subsequently, in June 1941, the British and Australian governments gave the Dutch Government in exile a private assurance that any attack from outside on a line running from Singapore to Australia via the Netherlands East Indies would be a mutual *casus belli*.

15   Netherlands East Indies.

16   Menzies omits closing bracket.

Approaching BIMA, in SOEMBAWA, get first clear views of native life—tiny terraced and irrigated allotments—no space wasted, and with all buildings and residences concentrated in villages. Same observed on vastly greater scale near Sourabaja in Java, where, at a busy post we are received by MICKLEREID, the British consul. Shedden, Storey & I dine with him in a house the entire floor of which is of marble, and so spacious that not surprised to learn it was built by Chinese millionaire at a cost of over £100 000. Shedden & I agree that British wise to give consuls such "prestige surroundings"—we must tell Jack Beasley[17] about it.

Before dinner have long talk at consulate with Governor (VAN DER PLAS) a handsome, active, and intelligent man whose face is partly hidden behind a straggling dark beard. He said some shrewd things worth noting—

Holland was overrun in 5 days, but had enough "empire sense" to transfer government to London; result, Dutch fleet colonial empire &c intact and belligerent. France made great mistake of not doing ditto because average Frenchman has no "Empire sense" and therefore forgot all save metropolitan France. Pétain, after this first error, has played his cards well.[18] In Holland, Winkelmann,[19] the pure soldier, surrendered his army. If he had possessed a political imagination and sense, he could have got out of Holland from the sector N. of Amsterdam (ship canal), thousands of soldiers & much equipment which would today revolutionise the defensive position of the Netherlands East Indies. Governor greatly admires British Empire sense, as shown in Empire Air Scheme.[20] Somewhat similar sense has prevented Holland from becoming a mere province like Denmark or Switzerland.

A long and rough day's flying; head winds keeping us low for most of journey. On whole, disappointed with flying comfort, a slight feeling of squeamishness is always present somewhere in the stomach.

---

17   John Albert Beasley, Labor member for West Sydney since 1928. As leader of the Lang Labor faction in the House of Representatives, he had earned the sobriquet of 'Stabber Jack' when he led his followers across the House in 1931 to destroy the Scullin Labor Government. For Menzies, he epitomised the extremest form of radicalism.

18   Marshal Henri-Philippe Pétain, veteran hero of the First World War, had in June 1940 formed the French Government which negotiated an armistice with the Germans. The Chamber of Deputies and the Senate, meeting in Vichy, conferred great powers on him as 'Chief of State'. In the unoccupied area of France he set up a paternalistic régime known thereafter as the Vichy Government whose motto was 'Work, Family and Fatherland', and which tried to steer an uneasy course between full and only partial collaboration with the Nazis.

19   Henri Gerard Winkelman, Commander-in-Chief of the Netherlands Army, Navy and Air Force.

20   The Empire Air Training Scheme, agreed to by Australia, New Zealand and Canada at the end of 1939, was set up to ensure a steady supply of Dominion airmen for war purposes in Europe. Elementary training was provided in their home countries followed by flying training in Canada.

<u>Tuesday Jany 28th</u>

Amazing view of intense cultivation, chiefly rice, as we fly across Java. An occasional oil well, a distant volcano; but chiefly rice—curiously shaped little terraces, millions of them; the peasants working in water; every few hundred yards, a village of say 50 or 100 cottages, surrounded by trees. From the 'plane window I can see at one time a hundred of such village oases. In some parts the practice is apparently quite communal—"to each according to his needs". Every time we pass over an area of the sea we see fish pens or traps shaped like arrow heads. So there we have the elementary economy of the Javanese—rice and fish. Our own easy-going agricultural methods in Australia seem quite unreal. How long can we safely keep them so?

Java 37,000,000 people on 50,000 sq miles (two thirds of the State of Victoria!) At Batavia,[21] received by Peterson (Aust. Govt. Commissioner, reported here to do well!) & Walsh, the Consul General, a contemporary of T.A.L. Davy at Exeter. Hurried visit to the Governor General, Jonkheer van Starkenborgh Stachouwer.

Young looking and handsome man of 52, looking like 38. In all internal matters, practically the dictator of the NEI—on foreign policy subject to Dutch Govt in London. Speaks perfect English and has an air-conditioned office at his white Palace! Very frank conversation in which he states his position as follows:

1.   He admits that there has in the past been an apparent ambiguity about his position, for the reason that he did not desire to provoke Japan, and hoped for the best.

2.   Of recent weeks he has become pessimistic. All his information points to an intensifying of Japanese demands and truculence. In present negotiations, Japs are demanding unrestricted immigration. They are not content with equal access to supplies of goods, but want Government to guarantee them certain volumes of supply.

3.   If Japan strikes, the Dutch will definitely resist. But they are short of arms, aircraft, and ammunition.

4.   These things led to agreement re staff talks, which he thinks should be complete detailed and searching. (He plainly has doubts as to whether they have been).

5.   Attaches great importance to joint declaration NEI, G.B., U.S.A., Australia, but thinks time not yet ripe. Must not be premature and

---

21   Now Jakarta.

provocative, but also must not be so late that Japan already committed and face therefore has to be saved.

6.   Disappointed with U.S.A, both on supply of war material and on expressions of policy, which he finds (as I do) too aloof.

My general impression very good; this man possesses strength of character. The local opinion grows in favour of G.B.—Churchill is a popular figure—and "Spitfire Funds" increasingly succeed.

<u>Wednesday Jan 29th</u>   Last night at Singapore most interesting. Time did not permit a visit to the base, which we saw from the air this morning. A car run along to the causeway to Johore—magnificent public buildings—fine gardens. But the interesting material at Singapore was human—and disturbing.

The governor, Sir Shenton Thomas, is compact, brisk and I should think efficient. Talks with precision and emphasis, instead of the usual vague phrases "d'you see what I mean" &c of the tropical service Englishman. His wife is small and intelligent, except that she races horses and sometimes wins. The new C in C.[22] of the Far East, Air Chief Marshall Sir Robert Brooke-Popham, looks like the late Baden-Powell. He has borne the white man's burden in many places from Kenya to Canada, and it has left his shoulders a little stooped. His hair and moustache are both sandy and wispy and a little indeterminate. He received us at the landing stage, wearing a pith helmet, a "bush shirt" of khaki, the tail outside the trousers in the manner of a tunic, & shorts. So complete a type was he that I had much ado not to say "Dr Livingston, I presume". His voice is thin and high pitched, but, after a while, not unpleasant. His attitude throughout our talks was courteous and benevolent, he is a first class listener, but he left me with a vague feeling that his instincts favour some heroic but futile Rorke's Drift[23] rather than clear-cut planning, realism and science.

Winston Churchill had lunched him in London before he came out to this appointment, and he was boyishly pleased that Winston's farewell exhortations to him had contained more than a hint of the forlorn hope ("Hold out to the last, my boy, God bless you. If your grandfather had not broken his neck playing polo at Poona he would be proud of you this day!").

General Bond commands the army, presumably. Tall, well-groomed, and with that form of mental hiccups which reduces conversation to a series of

---

22   Commander-in-Chief.

23   A celebrated battle in the Zulu War of 1879 in South Africa when, soon after a decimation at Isandhlwana of 1700 British troops by 20 000 Zulus, a forewarned garrison of 120 men at Rorke's Drift held off a similar flood of Zulu attackers. Paintings of this famous incident, which symbolised British gallantry, were common in Menzies' youth.

unrelated ejaculations. One eye is closed, the other droops behind a monocle. If there is action, the General will no doubt die gallantly, but too many of his men will die with him. Air Vice Marshall Babbington[24] commands the RAF. His information appeared sketchy and he also is of few words. Admiral Layton was easier and very human but he did not stay for our conference.

Several conclusions must be drawn from our talk after dinner:

1.　We are, in the Far East, grievously short of aircraft. Three squadrons of fighters, even Gladiators, would have a great deterrent effect upon Japan.

2.　The army problem is principally one of material, though a turned-over Australian Brigade Group would be "most helpful".

3.　The absence of naval craft must encourage the Japanese.

4.　If Japan is to take over Thailand and moves down the Malay Peninsula, we should push forward to a point already selected, even if it does mean a breach of neutrality.

5.　This Far Eastern problem must be taken seriously and urgently. [I at once sent instructions to Australia that three-cornered staff talks should occur at Singapore at once, so that results may be cabled to us in London].[25]

6.　Brooke-Popham is I gather active and a disciplinarian. He must ginger up these other people, who have a more garrison outlook. Why the devil these generals and people should be ignorant of and not interested in the broad principles of international strategy I cannot understand. All the talk on those aspects was by myself, with Shedden feeding me with material.

7.　We must as soon as possible tell Japan "where she gets off". Appeasement is no good. The peg must be driven in somewhere. I must make a great effort in London to clarify this position. Why cannot one squadron of fighters be sent out from N. Africa? Why cannot some positive committment be entered into regarding naval reinforcement of Singapore? At this stage, misty generalisations will please and sustain the Japanese, and nobody else.

Today, we fly high (10 000 ft) and cool and smooth—a pleasant change after the rough and hot journey we have so far had. Call at Penang, where local

---

24　　Air Vice-Marshal John Babington.

25　　Menzies to Fadden, 29 January 1941, *DAFP*, vol. IV, pp. 352–3.

Counsellor receives us (with Brigadier Lyon, formerly of Melb. Govt House) and we drive hurriedly to Penang Club. Houses, gardens, flowers, colours, all are delightful. I have never seen a prettier place. Earlier we flew over Kuala Lumpur, surrounded by great patches of dredged land.

At 5 pm arrive at Bangkok and received by Sir Josiah Crosby[26] & most of the Thailand mission to Australia. Chief impression driving to the Legation, is of sudden bad smells. Legation first class—a compound of buildings—the British certainly do their diplomatic people well. Crosby, about 64, is large, approachable, and genially despotic; has had 36 years in this part of the world and is clearly well regarded. The P.M. of Thailand has today accepted Japanese arbitration in the Indo Chinese affair; Crosby doubts whether Cabinet really approved, and is of course apprehensive that this means Japanese control of Thailand. This is bad for us, but British Foreign Office will not cease to cultivate friendships here; there is never any use in being schoolmasterly.

Crosby and I called on the PM at his closely guarded house. He is small, wore a dark green uniform, and struck me as both friendly and unhappy. Through an interpreter, I was chiefly concerned to emphasise by reference to what we are doing in Australia, the power and the unity of the British Empire. It is a good theme. These Thais don't want Japanese domination, but they just don't see how they can resist Japanese pressure. Crosby very caustic about (1) America which cut off war supplies to Thailand because, technically, she was the aggressor against French Indo China, and thus threw Thailand into the hands of Japan. (2) Vichy government, which has produced this trouble by being stiff-necked over a couple of worthless patches of land, without any real power to enforce the results of its obstinacy.

What a pity that the U.S.A. attitude should so frequently be so academic and so "preachy".[27]

Dinner at Legation—quite amusing—sherry, 1928 Nuits St Georges, Champagne—and Port would have been served with the slightest encouragement. "For though the English are effete, they're quite impervious to heat."[28]

---

26   Sir Josiah Crosby was British Minister in Thailand, 1934–41. (It was Siam until 1939.)

27   At this time there was a frontier dispute between Thailand and French Indo-China, and Japan offered mediation. Britain was anxious to keep Japan and Thailand apart lest, as in fact later happened, Japan use Thailand as a springboard for an attack on Malaya. But the United States took the high moral view that in the dispute Thailand was the aggressor, and cut off military supplies which had already been promised to the Thais. Vichy France was also, predictably enough, uncompromising. Crosby, in a dispatch of 1 February, bemoaned the fact that 'for six months Britain had been fighting a lone battle in Thailand, hampered rather than aided by those who should have cooperated with her'. Hasluck, p. 330.

28   A line from Noel Coward's song 'Mad Dogs and Englishmen'.

Mosquitoes are here so bad that beds are placed under permanent gauze screens, as are some groups of chairs and tables.

Very nice boy called Stuart (son of Percy Stuart of Melbourne) is on Legation staff. He was one of the party when I dined Joe Gullett at Oxford some years ago![29]

Query: What about sending one or two of our External Affairs men to places like this for a few month's experience?

Query: What about accrediting Latham to this place as well as Japan? Crosby suggests it.[30]

Thursday Jany 30th

Again fly high—to Rangoon, on the wide and muddy Irrawaddy. We do not leave the river—are received by various officials on a large steam launch, where we drink beer and feel cool. In the distance, the great gold pagoda is a striking thing, though we are modestly informed that "only the top 10 feet are solid gold!"

Akyab a remote sort of point, where we for the first time sit in a perfectly cool room at the Resident's house. Resident's (Wilkie?) wife is a West Australian.

Shades of evening are beginning to fall as we reach Calcutta, where we moor on the Hooghly (one of the mouths of the Ganges) near the great new Willingdon Bridge. In absence of Governor of Bengal (Sir J.A. Herbert) received by Col. Peel, his military secretary. Tom Wilson on the landing stage, & am able to give him pleasant messages. Had a drink with him and several Americans & wives at his house which is delightful. Dinner at G.H. Rather impressed by Maj. General Heydeman & Brigadier Wood who is D.G. of Supply, was very active in the Delhi Conference;[31] dark moustache, faintly Jewish looking and very clear headed and confident.

Bed (in the Prince of Wales Suite of a vast palace) late and to be called at 3.45 a.m! As I saw Calcutta only in the dark, my chief impression is one of confused lights, sprawling streets, and adventurous traffic.

---

29   Menzies' 1935 Diary of his first trip to England notes that he took Henry Baynton ('Jo') Gullett and some of his friends to dinner in Oxford on 17 May 1935. Francis H. Stuart, born in Australia, had become a member of the British Foreign Service.

30   Sir John Latham, Chief Justice of the High Court, had been appointed late in 1940 as the first Australian Ambassador to Japan.

31   The Eastern Group Supply Conference was held in New Delhi in October 1940. The aim of discussions there was to improve the organisation of war supplies to Empire forces in the Middle East, the Far East and India by coordinating the industrial efforts of Australia, New Zealand, South Africa, India, and the African and Asiatic colonies. Hasluck, p. 302.

Friday Jany 31st

Took off from the river by flares, and came out of my coma only at intervals during the day. Right across the greatest breadth of India—Allahabad (on the Jumna, near its confluence with the Ganges—a holy place of pilgrimage), Gwalior, on a lake, with low scrubby tiger country about it, Raj Samand, a lake and a great retaining wall, with steps cut down to the water, and a holy village on a hill, and some good talk from Commissioner Todd about Suttee and the like practices, and then Karachi—cool and civilised—our host Clee, Chief Secretary in the Sind administration, whose wife born in Australia. A cool Sind Club, with a fire burning in the smoke room!! where I witness a game of 'Slosh' and table bowls, played with billiard balls put along by hand with a skittle near Kitty—and minus 2 if you knock it over!

While we were within touch of the Ganges, the country looked marvellous. Every inch green & irrigated; houses built square about a courtyard; an occasional tree. As we proceeded west the country dried up, much of it quite arid looking. But wherever you go, you see in some moist corner of a mountain range, some remote valley, the gleam of a green and watered patch; terraced and irrigated, and sustaining its few of India's millions.

Saturday Feb 1st   Chiefly over desert foreshore—eroded and barren hills—and the Sea. First stop Jiwani in Baluchistan, where a guard of honour is produced. Splendidly got up Baluchi troops, who present arms with great snap.

[At Karachi East meets West—the Camel harnessed to a cart on rubber tyres—a fascinating sight]

Pass over sun-scattered rocky mountains of Eastern Arabia. The most desolate looking country I've seen. And yet, here and there, a little patch of cultivation—half an acre even—where some water has apparently been held in the rocks.

DUBAI, BAHREIN, BASRA all on the Persian Gulf but quite cool at 8000 ft.

Just remembered that at Karachi there were errors in decoding and Storey was described as "Commissioner of Aircraft Disarmament!" I must tell Hackett this.

Once more, at every stopping place, I am impressed by the cool, youngish, educated and good-looking Englishman who materialises, whether as Resident, Commissioner, Law Officer, adviser to the local Sheikh (pronounced SHAKE) or whatnot. These mysteries under which Englishmen hold posts of authority in non-British countries are quite beyond me, but the breed is superb. After all, if the system were simple and logical, the British probably would not have thought of it.

Bahrein—a flat city on flat sands by the side of the sea. Received by Commander Graham, whom I met once at 'Parkwood' with Clive Baillieu.[32] Bahrein—pearls and an oil refinery, which the Italians came over and tried to bomb about 2 mos ago. They missed by 500 yards. As Graham says, they "could have landed and pitched their bomb over the refinery fence", but they didn't. Before the war the buyers from places like Cartier's used to come out here and buy their pearls direct. No fear of a cultured or imitation pearl—their possession in this country is a crime.

Getting stuffier and more tired each day—a few days break in the Middle East will be welcome.

Approaching Basra, we pass over the enormous delta of the Euphrates and the Tigris, vast sandy flats, some showing the marks of drains to get the salt out of them. Then date palms—millions of them, on the flat. I discover at dinner that Australia is Iraq's chief date customer. Splendid port, aerodrome and hotel, all run by a small dynamic person Sir John Ward, who for 20 years has been railway chief, port authority, aerodrome builder &c &c &c for Iraq and wishes GB would take the place over. "Si monumentum requiris circumspice".[33] Dine at hotel as guest of Consul Weld-Forester. Also present Holman, Counsellor at Bagdad and good sprinkling locals. I make a speech emphasising the Empire and Australian effort. Iraq has been playing ambiguous game. P.M. resigned yesterday & we are hoping for a safer & more loyal government. Holman thinks sending a brigade of Australian troops via Basra wd be a good demonstration.

Shatt-al-Arab Hotel. Partridge, foie gras, chablis and Nuits St George— how odd. First black-out—queer to have no bedroom window open.

<u>Sunday Feb 2nd</u>   Basra—date palms—sandy delta. Tigris, Euphrates, semi-desert—a passage over Kut-Al-Amara, with the Barrage & water pouring through—Ctesiphon[34] with its curved roof and facade standing a solitary ruin. One of the seven wonders of the world—more sandy plains—mud huts with thatched roofs—goats, cattle, Bagdad in the distance—<u>Lake Habbaniyah</u>. There I

---

32   Clive Baillieu, the eldest son of W.L. Baillieu, who was known as 'Australia's money king', and was scion of the Collins House group of financiers. After serving with distinction in the First World War Clive became the head of the Baillieu interests abroad and on his father's death in 1939 took charge of all the family businesses. His friendship with Menzies arose from a range of common interests, legal and political, in the 1920s.

33   'Si monumentum requiris circumspice'—'If you seek a monument, gaze around'. Menzies is quoting the inscription in St Paul's Cathedral, London, attributed to the son of Sir Christopher Wren, its architect.

34   Ctesiphon, the ruined palace of the Sassanian (Persian) kings. But it was not one of the seven wonders of the world—it was not built until late Roman times. Special thanks are due to Mr Bob Barnes, of the Classics Department, Australian National University, for having identified this obscure and, in the end, incorrect reference.

meet Sir Basil Newton, British Ambassador at Bagdad (Iraq), who was at Prague at the time of Munich. Tall, droopy, homely looking: but extremely interesting on Iraq. The Regent is clear-headed but only 25, afraid of his advisers. P.M. cleared out yesterday, new man a stop gap, being a little better but not much. Newton thinks well of Benes[35]—not a 'twicer' (as Bruce thinks) but perhaps a trifle academic. All this Persian country does not suggest the golden days of the Arabian Nights or Omar Khayyam.

West across desert, Trans-Jordan. Rugged & mountainous, but as you approach Palestine every patch of soil or hillside or valley cultivated, fallow or green. "He leadeth me beside the still waters"—green pastures &c achieves significance. Then suddenly the Sea of Galilee and the lone green wonder of the Jordan valley. Received at Tiberias by Sir H. McMichael,[36] the H.C. for Palestine, & General Blamey.[37] Lunch & cameras. McMichael a scholar with no illusions about Jewish politicians but a respect for Jewish reclamation & agricultural achievements; no illusions about Arabs, who are double crossers par excellence, but a respect for their good manners & handsome appearance.

At upper end of Galilee, the village of Capernaum, and the slope of the Gadarene Swine. Drive to Jerusalem with Sir Harold McMichael. Amidst talk of the classics, philology and poetry (and incidentally the laws of economics, the existence of which McMichael wisely decries) we pass through lovely green and sacred country—Caria of Galilee, Nazareth—a fairly large town—Carmel, Samaria to Jerusalem. Surprising greenness. Perfect day. Curse because camera packed in bag, and bag in advance car. Dine at G.H.—lovely Arab architecture with arched ceilings. General Nime[38]—great admirer of John Dill.[39]

Whole day a most thrilling experience. Must get a map.

---

35   Eduard Beneš, President of the Czechoslovak Republic in exile. In 1938–39 Menzies, under the influence of British Foreign Office officials, thought that Beneš was unnecessarily prolonging tensions in Europe by refusing to accept Hitler's outrageous demands.

36   Sir Harold MacMichael, British High Commissioner in Palestine, which since 1922 had been a mandate under British rule. The Balfour declaration of 1917 had asserted that the then British Government 'viewed with favour the establishment in Palestine of a national home for the Jewish people': the history of Palestine thence became one of extreme tension between Jewish settlers and indigenous Arabs. When in the later 1930s Nazi persecution in particular created great numbers of Jewish refugees, ambivalent British policy attempted severely to limit Jewish immigration to Palestine, producing much consequent turmoil.

37   Lieutenant-General Sir Thomas Albert Blamey, Commander of the Australian Imperial Force.

38   Lieutenant-General Sir Philip Neame, General Officer Commanding Palestine, Trans-Jordan and Cyprus, 1940–41.

39   General Sir John Dill, Chief of the Imperial General Staff.

Monday Feb 3rd

From my bedroom window I can see, right to left, the folded mountains of Trans-Jordan, a glimpse of some village in the Jordan Valley, the Mount of Olives and the old walled city of Jerusalem, with the green slope on this side of the walls which denotes the garden of Gethsemane.

Further reflections upon yesterday. The Jews have done some great agricultural work here, heavily subsidised from abroad. The broad valley N.E. of Mount Carmel is a picture of brown and green—and a few years ago it was a swamp. The Jewish settlers would be content but for a few politicians. I should think that McMichael, a most cultivated soul, dislikes the Jews in the mass and has a sneaking regard for the Arab who "though he will shoot at you for the fun of it and double cross you as a matter of course, has the general bearing and attitude of a gentleman".

[A quaint combination on this sunny morning, for as I write there walk across the garden, with all this sacred geography behind it, 6 prisoners in brown, working in the garden & followed by an armed warden!!]

Further impression. Can these mandates really work. There is here a problem of reconciling Jew and Arab, which will become active again after the war. We, the mandators, have all the odium of attempting settlement & direction without the real power of government. McM. thinks, and I agree, that having regard to the strategical position of Palestine we should have cut out sentimentality long ago and taken it over.

In the morning I see the War Cemetery at Jerusalem—a really beautiful memorial of the local stone. Then, in company with Keith-Roach, the chief administrator on McMichael's staff, I go, via the Damascus Gate and the Jaffa Gate into the old city—down a quaint narrow street (David Street) with vendors of meat, cooked & cooking food, vegetables, &c, to the Mosque Omar. On the way, we dart into a side alley, where we see an inn (doors & a railing on the first floor) and below a stable, a manger on the Bethlehem model. Mosque Omar rich in mosaic and a little garish. Inside, the living rock occupies the centre—Mount Maria. Another mosque nearby. A queer concentration of Christian & Moslem, but of course the latter have always admitted Jesus a holy prophet, and Jerusalem is one of the three holy cities of the Mohammedans. We turn aside on the way to see the wailing wall of the Jews. Here are long black-haired Rabbis, some of whom collect fees for vicarious prayer. Roach, who has been here for many years, and enjoys the obvious respect of hundreds of passers by whose language (Arabic) he speaks with dignity and ease, tells me that e.g. a Jewish Stock-broker in New York will pay a Jerusalem Rabbi £15 p.a. to say so many prayers a day for him at the wailing wall!

From the boundary wall of the Mosque we look across the Garden of Gethsemane to the Mount of Olives (now crowned by a Russian Tower.[40] From a grille in the second Mosque we see the village of Siloam, threaded by the brook Kedron ("cool Siloam's shady rill").[41]

Thence a few miles to Bethlehem with the Church of the Nativity (350AD) entered by a "needle gate". Only indigenous craftsmanship is in mother of pearl and I secure a necklace for Heather.[42]

Press interview at Govt. House and then off with Blamey, who is in good shape and of high intelligence.

Call at Scottish Hospital, with red headed and elderly Scots matron at BEER YA'AGOV, (near Aramathea)[43] and see 100 or so Australian casualties from Bardia. All in good heart, and we exchange badinage. Thence to Railway Corps & Gaza. Cocktail party at Officers Mess—Fred Gamble[44] (very popular), McCausland, L.G. Male, Dunn, Norris, Laverack.[45] Miss Wilson, the Chief Matron, J.A. Norris's son, slightly wounded at Bardia &c &c. Dine in the Mess of H.Q. Base area—Brigadier Boase. A splendid day.

Tuesday Feby 4th

There is strange husbandry in this fertile looking country, which I am of course seeing at its best. Ploughing by a camel and a bullock hitched to a plough that is practically a bent stick with an iron point on it!

A great day's programme, driving around the camps—troops drawn up in many places—salutes—great precision—with only the old and bold cooks calling out "How are you Bob?"

At Julis Camp march past of 21st Brigade (J. Stevens—a good one) and RAA of 9th Aust. Div. With amplifiers I address them—a message of encouragement from Australia to them—a message from them to the gallant people of Great Britain—no cheap promises but a pledge that at home we will

---

40 Menzies omits closing bracket.

41 Hymn no. 583 in the Scottish Psalter (1929). 'By cool Siloam's shady rill/ How sweet the lily grows!/ How sweet the breath, beneath the hill, / Of Sharon's dewy rose!'

42 His daughter, then aged thirteen.

43 By 'Aramathea' Menzies probably means what is now the nearby town of Ramla, a town important in the Crusades as Rames, the headquarters of Richard Coeur de Lion, and the traditional site of the house of Joseph of Arimathea. The original Arimathea was north of Beer Ya'Agov, near the modern town of Ramatayim.

44 John Frederick Gamble had been, before the war, Chief Clerk and Assistant Parliamentary Draftsman in the Attorney-General's Department and had worked with Menzies ever since he became Attorney-General in 1934.

45 Major-General John Dudley Lavarack, General Officer Commanding Australian 7th Division, 2nd AIF.

endeavour to work for them so as to be worthy of them.[46] It is a moving thing to speak to thousands of young men, mere boys, in the flower of their youth, many of whom will never see Australia again. War is the abomination of desolation, but its servants are a sight to see. These men are unbeatable.

Lunch at Laverack's Div H.Q., where I see Berryman just back from Bardia.

Afternoon at Deir SUNEID, another march and speech on similar lines. Then to No 1 Aust Gen. Hospital, where I see many nurses, all cheerful, more sick & wounded (including, sick, P.R. Le Couteur's son George) &, among doctors, Lorimer Dodds[47] of Sydney. Blamey suggests we should send concert parties & entertainers from Australia—I will recommend this.

Go to a concert at night—good Jewish troupe, and speak at interval. Heckling dies down, and a splendid hearing. As we come out, air raid warning on and we drive with dimmed lights, threatened by every sentry.

Morshead[48] (new Major-General of 9 Div) arrives, looking first rate. Also meet Arthur Embling's son.[49]

Wednesday Feb 5th

Gaza to Lydda[50] airport—very modern & good. Just after we arrived, an air raid signal & we are asked to go to the air raid shelter. However, we decided to finish our aperitif, and as we sat down to lunch the "all clear" sounded. "Where ignorance is bliss, 'tis folly to be wise".[51] Fly by Lockheed with a fantastically good-looking R.A.F. pilot, Goodhead, to Heliopolis. Received by Sir Miles Lampson, the British Ambassador, large, shrewd and hearty as ever.

Cocktail at Australian Soldiers Club, a large house-boat on the Nile—Blamey and Lady B. hosts. See General Wavell, of few words & with sinister left eye[52]—Freyberg,[53] looking well, General Catroux, formerly of French Indo China.

---

46 'I promise and pledge you that Australia will be behind you through good and bad. We all know your sacrifices,' he told the men. 'I cannot describe the immense pride and affection felt for you at home. Go forward; you are not alone.' *Sydney Morning Herald*, 6 February 1941.

47 Major Lorimer Fenton Dods.

48 Major-General Leslie J. Morshead, General Officer Commanding Australian 9th Division, since 1 February 1941.

49 Arthur Embling was a long-standing member of both the Melbourne Stock Exchange Committee and Menzies' beloved Savage Club.

50 Now Lod.

51 Thomas Gray, 'Ode on a Distant Prospect of Eton College' (1747).

52 General Sir Archibald Percival Wavell, from 1939 British Commander-in-Chief for the Middle East. Of him John Colville notes: 'He was shy and not good at expressing himself orally, so that Churchill never grasped his best qualities.' *Fringes*, p. 576.

53 Major-General Bernard Cyril Freyberg, Commander of the New Zealand Expeditionary Force.

Lady Lampson vivacious as ever.[54] Dinner at night at Embassy. The new Egyptian P.M. HUSSEIN SIRRY PASHA, an uncle of King Farouk's wife: speaks fluent English, amusing, intelligent. We find political problems are the same the world over—and laugh over them. Other house guests, Lord & Lady Glenconner, Capt Hon T. Cope—12th generation descendant of Sir Edward Cope (and has read Cope on Littleton) and one Channon MP from London—agreeable but indeterminate. Sir Arthur Longmore at dinner.[55]

Things in Egypt have improved—the P.M. is friendly and Libyan victories have done their job. But today a ship was mined in the Suez Canal—the Germans having laid some by aeroplane. One German is worth 15 Italians.

Thursday Feby 6th

To the Palace, to sign the books of the King, Queen and Queen Mother. At the Palace, saw the Chef de Cabinet (Liaison between King & P.M.—adviser to King) AHMED HASSANEIN PASHA, a slightly built, ascetic looking man, educated in England, a pioneer of aviation & a noted explorer. He is completely friendly to the British, and listened with obvious pleasure to a short account of what we are doing in Australia. His influence with Farouk would be greater if he had more strength of will. I am to see the King next Monday. On all sides they tell me (and nobody more plainly than Sirrey[56] Pasha) that Farouk is behaving badly. There is an indifferent family history both physical & mental. This boy had just been sent to England under the tutelage of Hassanein a few months before Fuad's death, and consequently his education, only beginning, came to an end. Self willed, flattered, with no mental discipline, he is, at 21, a problem. Lady Lampson describes him as frequently "naughty, like a school boy, being rude to the masters!" He dislikes the company of diplomats or thinkers, and makes boon companions of servants. His place is on the throne but his instincts take him to the servants hall. The previous P.M., ALI MAHEB, was his creature. As a limited monarch, his powers are legally small, but as Sirrey told me today, he can, by interference and intrigue, do a great deal of harm.

Paid a call on the P.M., and received one in return. Two most interesting talks. I like this man immensely. He is an irrigation engineer of great standing, a

---

54   The admiration here was mutual. When Menzies left, Lady Lampson wrote in a farewell note: 'Noone cd have been a more charming or easy guest—or a wittier! <u>Come back soon</u>.' 13 February 1941, Menzies Family Papers.

55   Henry ('Chips') Channon, American-born Conservative MP, also described the occasion in his diary: 'There was an impressive dinner party at the Embassy to meet Mr Menzies, the Australian Prime Minister. He is jolly, rubicund, witty, only 46 with a rapier-like intelligence and gifts as a raconteur.' *Chips*, p. 290.

56   Usual spelling is Sirry—Menzies varies.

good administrator and completely honest. He dislikes demagogues & is therefore not too popular with the Wafd;[57] like myself, he believes that "whatever is best administered is best". It was amazing to find so much common ground in conversations which ranged over Budgets, stamp duties, income tax, War Time Profits Taxes (Egypt is doing famously—a bulk sale of the cotton harvest, and £2 000 000 a month spent by soldiers), questions without notice, quorums & counting out, and Parlty procedure generally. One interesting practice here is that Ministers may and regularly do attend and speak in either House, but may vote only in their own.

Press interview—a success. The first Dominion P.M. they had ever seen. Spokesman assured me of their faith in British victory. Interesting to discover, however, that some propaganda already going on here to effect that Egyptian help to G.B. is so great (though they have not declared war on Italy—merely broken off diplomatic relations!) that after war Egypt should be called to the Peace Conference and, presumably, given a share of the loot.

At lunch today, saw Mrs Hore-Ruthven and Hermione Ranfurly—full of beans though an "illegal wife" ie a wife of a serving officer, not supposed to be here at all.

Tonight I dine with Blamey at the Turf Club. Wavell, Longmore, Lampson, CATROUX (French I-C),[58] et hoc genus omne[59] present. I speak, fortunately in my best form and the result seems encouraging to these Generals & Marshals.

Friday Feb 7th

Today to Alexandria across the Delta—that miracle of close cultivation, intersected by canals, and ending most abruptly at the sands of the desert. At Alexandria, inspect what was Morshead's Brigade—from England. A good deal of dust blowing—they acclimatise them for the desert at this camp. Tents are scattered irregularly and about 80 yards apart. This vastly spreads out a unit, but it is a sound protection against bombing raids. Then to the fleet, where I meet Admiral Cunningham[60]—slim, red faced, blue eyed, radiating optimism, faith in his ships and his men. This is the No 1 personality I have so far encountered on this journey: compared to him Chatfield[61] is a stuffed clothes man. Sad to see French warships in port—neat but useless. Go on board Stuart (Capt Waller),

---

57   Wafd—the 'Al-Wafd Al-Misri' or Egyptian Delegation. A Nationalist Egyptian political party which had been instrumental in gaining Egyptian independence from Britain, and which continued to play a dominant role in Egyptian politics.

58   French Indo-China.

59   'Hoc genus omne'—'All that tribe', Horace, Satires, book 1, no. 2, 1.2.

60   Admiral Sir Andrew Cunningham, Commander-in-Chief of the Mediterranean since 1939.

61   Lord Chatfield, Admiral of the Fleet.

<u>Voyager</u> (where I also see <u>Vampire</u> men) and <u>Perth</u> (Bowyer-Smyth). These ships are doing wonderful service. Crews very fit and astonishingly young. Waller,[62] who has several submarines to his credit, is becoming almost as well known as Collins of the Sydney.[63] On these ships, as with the troops, the first question is "How are they in Australia?"; and when I answer "First Rate", there is a look of relieved pleasure, as if I had carried a personal message from each individual home. I must remember this—it is quite irrational, but human.

Lunch on <u>Warspite,</u> the Admiral's flagship, where I encounter Sir Charles Madden (whom I travelled with on the Strathaird in 1936). He is a Commander at 33 and as keen and boyish as ever. Warspite was through the bombing near Malta and Cunningham has a great story to tell. Then to <u>Illustrious</u> aircraft carrier, 8 times hit by 1000 lb bombs at Malta—the hangar and lifts knocked about, but steamed to Alexandria at 26 knots! Hats off to the ship-builders. For a week at Malta she was strafed, and the crew became very weary. So (and this is the secret of leadership in the R.N.) the men were relieved and the officers manned the pom-poms on the top deck and fought the dive-bombers all day!

Thence to Aust. Comforts Fund Hostel[64] at Alexandria (the bulk of which seemed dirty, with traffic going as you please on either side of the road), where I see Major McDonald, friend of Betty Fairfax.[65] Drink some Ballarat beer with the boys. And so fly back to Cairo, where there is a reception by Wavell & dinner at his house, en famille. I like Wavell, but with his left eye closed and his almost unbreakable silence he is an almost sinister figure. Everyone agrees that he is able, but this Libyan campaign has been entirely directed by General O'Connor, with brilliance and success. Its success (Bhengazi has fallen) is complete, and its speed almost beyond comprehension. At least 10 Italian Divisions defeated by 1 armoured & 1 infantry division.

<u>Saturday Feby 8th</u>

Today to the Western Desert, in pursuit of the 6th Division. Fly 500 miles of desert. See in distance Mersa Matruh and Sidi Barrani. Near the latter, the

---

62   Captain Hector M.L. Waller, DSO.

63   Captain John Augustine Collins, of HMAS *Sydney* and Assistant Chief of Naval Staff since 1939. Collins had been awarded a CB for brilliant Naval Action of HMAS *Sydney* July 1940 against the Italian cruiser *Bartolomeo Colleoni* in the Mediterranean.

64   The Australian Comforts Fund, formed in January 1940 from existing State funds and organisations, provided amenities to the Australian troops ranging from hostels, clubs and canteens both within Australia and overseas, to Christmas hampers and embarkation kits. The ACF acted in conjunction with the YMCA, the YWCA and the Salvation Army, with field commissioners operating overseas to coordinate the work of depots and the distribution of goods.

65   Betty Fairfax, the wife of Warwick Fairfax, proprietor of the *Sydney Morning Herald*, and a good friend of Menzies.

outline of fortified posts, and an occasional abandoned vehicle. The escarpment becomes visible, about 30 miles from the sea, closing in on it at about Sollum. Sidi Barrani is today a mere mark on the map, Sollum is a small village. So is Bardia, perched on high ground. But at Bardia there was obviously great fortification. A most amazing sight is seen here—in every Wadi or depression hundreds and hundreds of abandoned Italian vehicles. Altogether today I saw thousands! This Italian army had great numbers, superb equipment (our people had only about 100 field guns of light pattern in all), long prepared & well-placed defences, the skill of which everyone admits. All except guts!

We circle around Bardia twice—the sea brilliantly blue green and the land an orange yellow—quite superb from the air. As we fly over this barren country—completely bare rocky gravelly soil—we see occasionally the brown outline of some plot cultivated hastily by some Bedouins after a rain. Here also one sees occasionally the round brown mound which marks some old Roman cistern, used for water or grain storage underground. Shades of "Beau Geste".[66] Several large ones have been used as Italian headquarters in the field.

In Bardia harbour several sunken ships could be seen in the water. And so to Tobruk, where the vast perimeter of the defences, about 20 miles, could be seen, tank-traps & all, as if drawn on paper. Abandoned guns, tanks, lorries. Large stores of provisions in Tobruk itself. In Tobruk Harbour, 36 ships sunk or half sunk—here and there the foremast propping out of the water; the crane unused; the wireless masts standing drunkenly; a sad picture of what war means. This morning an inward bound tanker was mined, and it is now blazing merrily near the wharf. The naval men here consider the mines laid by German aircraft who raided the place two nights ago, and, they tell me for my comfort, may come again tonight. N.B. Torch provided, and shown the way down to the Air Raid Shelter.

I inspect and speak to 2 Battalions of Allen's Brigade—one in a wadi leading down to a decent beach—and the Anti-Tank Company, with 20 Italian tanks to their credit.

They all look splendid, but craving for news of home, and boyishly pleased when I pointed out the world significance of the campaign they have been winning.[67] At these speeches, I had a "sit down and smoke" order given and it was a success. "Tubby" Allen seems solid, with some good battalion commanders (England & Chiltern).[68] Godfrey, who has just become Acting Brigadier is fit, cheerful & has, I am told, done well.

---

66   'Beau Geste', a famous novel and 1920s silent melodrama about three English brothers who joined the Foreign Legion and heroically fought the Arabs in the desert.

67   'More than anything, the proud news of your triumph has bound Australia together in the war effort ... I congratulate you on your splendid deeds.' *Sydney Morning Herald*, 11 February 1941.

68   Lieutenant-Colonel Frederick Oliver Chilton.

Menzies farewells family and colleagues at Rose Bay, Sydney, before boarding the Qantas Empire Flying Boat Corinna. (Australasian, 26 April 1941)

Barbed wire entanglements offer scant protection to shipping on the waterfront in Singapore. (AWM 8497)

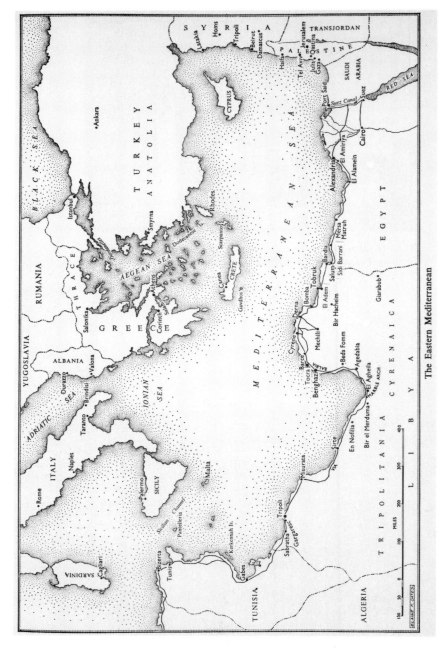

The Eastern Mediterranean

Adapted from Tobruk and El Alamein, *by Barton Maughan* (Courtesy AWM)

Landing at the Sea of Galilee, Lake Tiberias, in Palestine, Menzies is followed up the gangway by the Commander of the AIF, Lieutenant-General Sir Thomas Blamey, and the British High Commissioner, Sir Harold MacMichael, who received him. (Menzies Papers)

'Thumbs up' for the Prime Minister from Australian troops at the Soldiers Club, an Australian Comforts Fund hostel in Jerusalem. (Menzies Papers)

Visiting the War Cemetery at Jerusalem, Menzies is accompanied by Lieutenant-General Blamey, Frederick Shedden and Major Fred Gamble. (Menzies Papers)

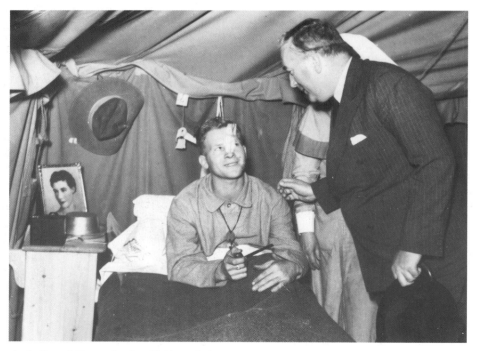

At the Scottish Hospital at Beer Ya'Agov, Palestine, Menzies meets one of the Australian casualties from the Bardia battle. (Menzies Papers)

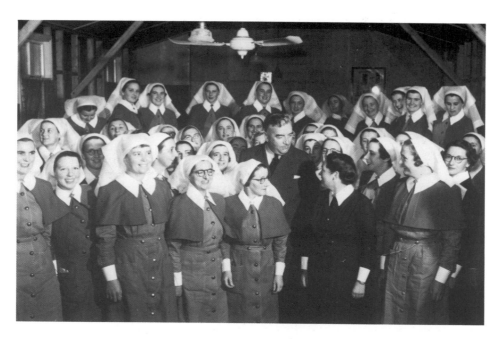

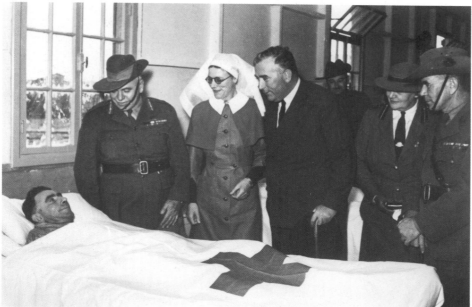

At Gaza Ridge Military Hospital nurses give Menzies a cheerful welcome (top) and (below) Menzies and Lieutenant-General Blamey visit a wounded soldier. (Menzies Papers)

With the British High Commissioner in Palestine, Sir Harold MacMichael, in Menzies' eyes 'a most cultivated soul'. (Menzies Papers)

At Julis, Palestine, Menzies stands to attention while Lieutenant-General Blamey takes the salute. (Menzies Papers)

'Eyes right' as Australian troops march past at Deir Suneid, Palestine. (Menzies Papers)

Menzies reviews the crew of an Australian warship, the Perth, *serving with the British fleet at Alexandria harbour.* (Menzies Papers)

Menzies and Lieutenant-General Blamey exchange pleasantries with a group of Australian soldiers. (Menzies Papers)

In Tobruk harbour a burning oil tanker, holed by a mine, provides a dramatic subject for Menzies' cine-camera. (Menzies Papers)

Menzies' plane circles over the small village of Bardia, scene of the Australian troops' first victory. (Menzies Papers)

Menzies inspects the ruins of Tobruk with Major Fred Gamble, a former colleague from his days as Attorney-General, now serving in the Middle East. (Menzies Papers)

Brigadier 'Tubby' Allen, Menzies and Brigadier Wootten, at Tobruk. (Menzies Papers)

After having the 'sit down and smoke' order given, Menzies addresses members of the 1st Australian Anti-Tank Company in the desert near Tobruk. (Menzies Papers)

At dinner at the British Embassy, hosted by Sir Miles Lampson (second from left), Menzies chats with Hussein Sirry Pasha, the Prime Minister of Egypt and his elegant wife. (Menzies Papers)

Arriving at El Adem, Menzies is met by Lieutenant-General Blamey. (AWM 6121)

Tobruk is a sizeable village with a good port, but must have been, like Bardia, a purely military settlement. There is no habitable hinterland. What I cannot understand is why the Italians, who boasted of Libya as an "Empire", and have spent hundreds of millions on stores, fortifications, buildings, the coast road, periodical memorials to Mussolini, motor equipment, &c, &c, &c, should have abandoned the whole show at the first attack of a mere fraction of their numbers.

Several officers send greetings to Anthony Eden,[69] who made a great mark in the Middle East.

N.B. Only trees growing at Tobruk are Gum Trees!

There are few shell craters—apparently the navy used a sensitive fuse which gave the greatest possible degree of fragmentation—and surprisingly little structural damage; but almost every wall is heavily pitted by flying fragments.

The administrative buildings are, of course, in the Plaza Benito Mussolini, and on the hospital wall is the proud slogan "Nothing is impossible". The whole of this area is a vivid illustration of the futility and pretentiousness of the facade of Dictatorship. "Sawdust Caesar" is a splendid title. A slogan is a poor substitute for a resolute will. I'm not sure that the abolition of maps would not improve the peace of the world. The sweating taxpayers of Italy probably thought Libya was worth it, because it looked fine and large when painted the Italian colour on the map!

See Douglas Pain[70] (Stamps Controller Vic) and Bridgford,[71] who send warm greetings to Frank.[72] Before dinner, I wander about the streets, chatting to various groups of AIF—a dash of humour is the right solvent, and they are friendly boys wise now in terrible things. It is cold here in the wind and our fellows wear a leather tunic over their uniform. They came on so steadily under fire that the Italians reported that they were wearing bullet proof mail shirts.

Capt. Frank Hurley, wearing Antarctic ribbons, is with us all the time, and I find him a splendid fellow indeed, with a great reputation for courage.[73]

Sunday Feb 9th   A great disappointment. Waken (no air raid) to the sound of heavy rain. News comes that aerodromes westward are flooded, and not possible

---

69   Anthony Eden, Secretary of State for Foreign Affairs, had recently visited the area.

70   Brigadier Duke Douglas Paine, Deputy Director of Supply and Transport.

71   Brigadier William Bridgeford, Australian Deputy Adjutant and Quartermaster-General.

72   Menzies' brother Frank was the Crown Solicitor of Victoria. Paine, Bridgeford and Frank Menzies were contemporaries and had spent their early schooldays together in Ballarat.

73   Official photographer with the AIF in the Middle East, Hurley had by this time something of a legendary status. He had accompanied Mawson and then Shackleton to the Antarctic, had been a crack photographer with the Australian forces in the First World War, and pioneered documentary film making in Australia between the wars.

to go to Benghazi or near it. So I must back to Cairo. But they promise me that if I come out again on Tuesday I can get through. So renewed hope. I must not miss seeing these men.

Drive from Tobruk to GAMBUT, a H/Qrs & aerodrome half way to Bardia, where the cold is so sharp that the R.A.F. men are wearing sheepskin overalls. Meet Clowes at Corps H/Qrs. Lunch with 113 Squadron of RAF (Blenheims)—cheery fellows—who give me an Italian air force plate—(how well these Italian officers did themselves in every way)—They call on me for a few words, and I thank the RAF on behalf of Australia.

And so, beaten temporarily by the weather, back by air to Cairo in 2³/4 hours!

The whole party are of opinion, and I myself feel, that this journey has been of great value and quite successful—beyond my expectations.

Tonight, dinner with Sir Arthur Longmore, the C in C of Air Forces in the Middle East. Winston Churchill broadcasts, to the pleasure of all save myself. No doubt Winston is right to appeal to the lowest common denominator among men—a hymn of hate—"the black hearted, treacherous Italians" &c, but I am quite sure we have a loftier cause than the one his speeches indicate.[74] Perhaps I am a little sour, for I have just read of Malcolm McDonald's removal to Canada as High Commissioner! I fear that Winston likes Yes Men; we shall have Brendan Bracken as a Minister next![75]

Monday Feby 10th   Prepare a broadcast, and then to my old friend Prince Mohamed Ali, who is pro-British, critical of our easy-going treatment of known enemy agents in Iraq and Egypt, but a complete believer in our victory.

Lunch with P.M. at Zafarani Palace, Madame Sirry Pasha good looking and bright. Mary Colebatch present, looking splendid in blue uniform with red tie.

---

74   Channon recorded his impressions on the same occasion: 'After dinner we listened to the Prime Minister's broadcast which was none too well received, particularly his references to the Middle East. Then Wavell, who knew what was coming, hid behind a doorway. As the Churchillian compliments to him were handed out that magnificent language seemed rather forced, almost comic. I was embarrassed as the only English politician present.' *Chips*, p. 291.

75   Malcolm MacDonald, the son of Ramsay MacDonald, was Secretary of State for Dominion Affairs in the mid-1930s and a friend made in Menzies' earlier trips to England. But he was identified with Chamberlain's appeasement policies, had negotiated with de Valera the handing over to Eire of the 'Treaty Ports' in 1938, and was reviled by Churchill who, as Menzies notes, moved him sideways by appointing him as British High Commissioner to Canada. Brendan Bracken, after an unruly boyhood in Ireland and adolescence in Australia, became controller of some important British financial papers, most notably the *Financial News*, and a member of the House of Commons at the age of twenty-nine. One of a small circle of intimates whom Churchill gathered around himself, almost like an inner court, Bracken did indeed subsequently become a minister, replacing Alfred Duff Cooper as Minister of Information in July 1941.

After lunch, talk with Wavell at M.E. Headquarters

(a)   Tripoli probably not worth while

(b)   Aggregation principle for AIF good, but must not be too rigid—eg guarding Canal or tackling Dodecanese. Difficult to find a front which will occupy entire Corps

(c)   Victory at Keren and Massawa would end East African campaign

(d)   Thinks we should consider forming a Second Corps Headquarters.

Make a broadcast to BBC,[76] and dine at Mohamed Ali Club with Mrs Hore-Ruthven, "Hermy" Ranfurly and Major Geoff Harford. And so to bed.

Tuesday Feby 11th

Out again to western desert. At El Adem (near Tobruk) pick up Blamey. At Bomba we circle over the drome, and three Hurricanes come up to escort us to Benghazi. Circle over B., an attractive white city. Received by some old friends, Stan Savige, Ned Herring,[77] G.A. Vasey, General Mackay, whose tactics are highly praised, but who looks as gently ineffectual as ever. The face is not the index of the man. Visit artillery officers & then address rank & file of artillery. Good interjections & good reception. Then to a picturesque barracks, with really lovely camouflage on the walls where I address a battalion of Infantry. Meet Brig. "Red" Robertson, a born salesman and propagandist with great tales of the Generals and Admirals he has captured. Blamey said later—"Robertson is a competent fellow, but he has won the war about three times already". Dine at Italia Hotel, after driving about and seeing a fine domed Church & many buildings of agreeable architecture and colour texture. At dinner, sit next to O'Connor the General who commanded the Corps. He did this job, but Wavell has received all the credit. A small, refined, alert man of immense charm, he does not look like the driving leader; but all present agree on enthusiastic regard for him. Wavell will probably get a peerage while this man gets a CB but that is the way of the world.

Discussion with Blamey regarding Wavell's points recorded above. His answers are—1. Australian forces must be regarded as national, under national command. This does not exclude the use of smaller units in special places, but all

---

76   Menzies' message on behalf of the Australian fighting men abroad and the people of Australia was: 'We know what this fight is about; we believe in its justice ... We solemnly vow that while we have any strength in us the people of Britain will not fight alone.' And to the people at home he said, 'The soldier in the front line here and the man in the Australian workshop are brothers in arms. Each must play his part.' *Sydney Morning Herald*, 12 February 1941.

77   Brigadier Edmund Herring and Menzies had been close political associates and friends since they campaigned together as young men in 1927. Herring became a Temporary Lieutenant-General in August 1941 and took command of the 6th Division.

must be subject to consent of G.O.C.[78] AIF. "If you give these English Generals an inch, they'll take an ell".

2. Premature to talk of a second corps, but will keep me posted in good time for training of corps personnel.

Impressions. Ned Herring cheerful, fit and first class. He should be a divisional commander soon, and may very well become a Corps Commander. He has flexibility of mind, imagination, and humour—rare qualities in military circles.

Benghazi goes along. What a tribute to a British conquest. Nobody dispossessed, no loot: good Australians slapping down their money on the bar of an hotel conducted by a "conquered" Italian.

Once in bed, I wage a losing warfare with man-eating mosquitoes.

Wednesday Feb 12th

Rise at 6.30, just dawn, and as I prepare to shave a series of explosions from near harbour, about 500 yards away. Some minelaying bomber, and AA[79] guns try a few shots. My first Air Raid.

Breakfast—bad coffee & dry bread. Series of addresses to infantry, from TORCA[80] to BARCE, including Louch's Battalion[81] (where I see "Private Biggins F" in the flesh) and Savige's Brigade.[82] The visit seems to have done good. There was some resentment that neither Spender nor Sturdee went west of Alexandria.[83] From near Benghazi to Barce we pass through a wide green valley, with a 2 year old "Cooperative Libyan Colony"—white concrete farms about 3/8 mile apart—a limestone soil recently cultivated—but the whole thing so scrupulously drawn in straight lines as to be rather depressing. A few farms deserted. There will be a problem of feeding these local people. At Barce, before entering a freezing & lumbering Valencia plane, top speed 85 mph!, meet General "Jumbo" Wilson.[84]

---

78 General Officer Commanding.

79 Anti-Aircraft.

80 This seems to be a mistake for Tocra (now Tukrah).

81 Brigadier T.S. Louch recorded that when Menzies visited the troops and spoke at a church parade at Tocra, 'the staff were anxious that he should not know how badly off we were for clothing, so the orders were that only the best dressed men should be in the front ranks. I was as tattered as anyone and had to be careful not to turn my back on him at any time.' Information by courtesy of Ken Johnson, Ardross, and *The 2/11th (City of Perth) Australian Infantry Battalion 1939–45* (1984), p. 50.

82 'If in the next few months I can feel that I have done half as good a job as you chaps have, I will be a proud and happy man,' he concluded his last speech. *Sydney Morning Herald*, 14 February 1941.

83 Percy Spender, Minister for the Army, and Lieutenant-General Vernon A. Sturdee, Chief of the Australian General Staff, had visited the Middle East early in January to confer with Blamey.

84 Lieutenant-General Sir Henry Maitland Wilson, Commander-in-Chief of the British Forces in Egypt.

Not impressed. All complaints about the "irregular" conduct of Australians on camp & guard duty, and nothing about their great fighting. Only one of whole bunch who intelligently understands is O'Connor. Wilson seems tall, fat and cunning.

At El Adem, we resume in the Lockheed Lodestar, and so "home" to Cairo—weary but satisfied.

El Adem is one of the many Italian aerodromes, splendidly equipped, along this coast. On our way out, a fire broke out in one hangar, and we wrote off a fine Blenheim by fire!

<u>Thursday Feb 13th</u> Write letters home, and then for an hour to the Bazaar, accompanied by Mrs Michael Wright,[85] Channon MP—staying here, and Madame Sirry Pasha. Purchase a piece of Russian jewellery for Pat, which the experts say is OK.[86] Lunch at Embassy with Col. Donovan,[87] after making a film for Hurley in the garden.

Then to Helwan to a N.Z. Hospital, where I see, talk to, and shake hands with 200 Australian wounded—all palpably pleased to hear a voice from home, and all amazingly cheerful. "Did you see my battalion? How are they? I'd love to be back with them!"

Race back to interview with War Correspondents and then to a reception by Payne at the Turf Club, attended by C.V. Hughes, back from Turkey. A representative collection of the British community, who listen eagerly to a speech by me on Australia's war effort. Some N.Z. officers present, obviously disgruntled with their own government, and green with envy of what we are doing. "A prophet is never without honour save in his own country & among his own people".[88]

Back at 8 pm to an interview with Wavell, who is clearly contemplating the possibility of a Salonika expedition.[89] Dinner at 9.30. We leave tomorrow.

I have worked like a nigger for these 10 days, but I think the results may be of great value.

---

85   Mrs Michael Wright, wife of Michael Robert Wright, Deputy Special Commissioner in South-East Asia, British Embassy in Cairo.

86   Channon recorded in his diary: 'Menzies wanted to buy a present for his wife and at last decided upon an emerald brooch in the shape of a peacock. There was much Eastern haggling and at last I got it for him for £45. He was enchanted.' *Chips*, p. 291.

87   Colonel William J. ('Wild Bill') Donovan, American lawyer of Irish extraction and First World War hero. At this time he was a roving agent for President Roosevelt and was shortly to have an important impact on Menzies when they met at Chequers on 9 March and discussed the problems of Ireland. Donovan was *persona grata* with the British Secret Service and was the founder of what ultimately became the CIA. On Donovan's colourful career, see Thomas F. Troy, *Donovan and the CIA* (Maryland, 1981), pp. 23–42; Anthony Cave Brown, *The Last Hero: Wild Bill Donovan* (New York, 1982), pp. 147–55; William Casey, *The Secret War Against Hitler* (Washington, 1988), pp. 14–17.

88   Matthew 13:57.

89   The only reference in the Diary to any discussion between Menzies and Wavell about a possible expedition to assist Greece. See Appendix I 'The Greek Campaign'.

Friday Feb 14th

Off to Khartoum, leaving a sorrowing Fred Gamble at Heliopolis: he is in great form. After a strenuous programme I snooze all the way to Wadi, and thence to Khartoum, where we are received by Sir Hubert Huddleston & wife (G.G.). They were on the "Strathmore" in 1938. The Palace is very fine, on the banks of the Blue Nile. Built by Kitchener on the site of the original house where Gordon[90] lived and was murdered. They tell me here that Gordon was of indomitable energy and quick temper. He was alone for all purposes most of the time. The Nile makes good gardens, and we enjoy an hour or two in a green spot. Before going to bed, hear across the river the irregular beat of the tom-tom and the wailing of the kind of flute that the snake-charmer uses. If Khartoum were not so modern and the row of houses and offices along the river so magnificent, it would be quite weird to hear these noises.

Last thing, news comes that the flying boat will be late at Lagos so we shall stay at Khartoum an extra day.

Saturday Feb 15th   We have struck Khartoum at the only cool time of the year and the extra day has proved a winner. In the morning, we drive across the river to the ordnance stores run by a long, dried-up looking Major Foley[91] (whose wife is charming!). When war broke out he had 150 men (including about 3 Europeans): now he has nearer 1500. He repairs machine guns, rifles & Brens; makes clothing for the troops; web equipment; leather bandoliers, camel & mule saddles; tables & other furniture; motor truck bodies; armoured cars; mills flour in a flour mill; robes of honour for native chiefs; repairs motor transport of all kinds; makes and camouflages tents; keeps large stores of spare parts; does the printing for the Soudan government & army; &c &c &c. "Housekeeping" good, and everybody works hard from 6.30 am to 6 pm, with a half hour off for breakfast & same at 2 pm for lunch. Wages 1/- to 1/6 per day. All problems tackled and most solved.

In afternoon, we go to city and battlefield of Omdurman (cf "The Four Feathers") and visit the residence of the Khalifa, the son of the Mahdi whose

---

90   General Charles George Gordon, who had in the late 1870s served as Governor-General of the Sudan under the Khedive of Egypt, was sent again by the British Government in 1884 to evacuate Egyptian forces from the capital, Khartoum. Khartoum was under attack from Sudanese rebels, led in a jehad by a Muslim mystic, the Mahdi. In January 1885 the Mahdists captured the town and massacred Gordon and the defenders. To the British public he became a murdered saint. 'Gordon' was in consequence a popular Christian name: it was, for example, after this heroic general that Menzies received his middle name.

91   Major Guy Francis Foley, Director of Stores and Ordnance, Controller General of War Supply, and Director of Economics and Trade in the Sudan Government.

Dervish followers killed Gordon.[92] The house is as much a Gordon museum as anything. What a man Gordon was—alone most of the time, and incapable of fear. In evening, call on various officials in spacious houses along the river, including one Forwood, who rowed with Dick Casey[93] at Cambridge in 1911, when, according to a silver cup, Dick rowed No 3 and weighed 11 stone 12 lbs. These officials educated, full of the genius loci. 3 mos leave p.a. in normal times and retire on decent pension at 50. This is worth considering for our colonial service in Papua & New Guinea.

N.B. At Omdurman one sees the memorial to the 21st Lancers, near the dip or KHOR through which they charged to intercept the retreating forces of the Khalifa. Among them a young man—Winston Churchill! We climbed up Surgham Hill & from there could see the whole plain from the Kerreri Hills at the North to the city of Omdurman in the South.

END OF DIARY 'A'; DIARY 'B' BEGINS

Sunday Feby 16th
 Go out and take a picture or two of Gordon on his dromedary: but fear that something has gone wrong with the camera.

Meet the two Princes, the sons of Haile Selassie. Nice lads, the younger one just out of Wellington School in England. Chapman Andrews—who amused me in 1938 from Suez to Cairo, is now adviser to Haile Selassie and is away to Abyssinia.

Meet a small Australian colony, including an Air Force Doctor Palfreyman, nephew of A.W. Palfreyman.[94]

Away to EL FASHER, a real native village. Fairly flat plains with hills & mountains suddenly emerging from them as if modelled & stuck on. Governor (of   Province) Ingleson[95]—Oxford—house was residence of Sultan— dining room four stands high up in corners where stood four women with lamps.

92　At the Battle of Omdurman, in September 1898, the British General Kitchener defeated the forces of the Mahdi's successor, the Khalifa, in the latter's capital, inflicting great losses and bringing the whole Mahdist movement to an end. 'The Four Feathers' was a silent movie of the popular book by A.E.W. Mason, in which a young army captain who resigns instead of going to the war in the Sudan receives four white feathers for cowardice from three of his brother officers and his fiancée. He proceeds to Egypt alone, bravely rescues each of the three officers in turn, and sends back the white feathers. Menzies, whose failure to volunteer in the First World War had prompted bitter public and private accusations of cowardice, may well have identified with the hero.

93　Richard Casey, formerly a Cabinet colleague, had been since March 1940 Australia's first Minister to the United States.

94　Achalen Woolliscroft Palfreyman, prominent Melbourne businessman and mining company director.

95　Menzies has left a space here; Philip Ingleson was the Governor of Darfur Province, Sudan.

Coloured roof beams—just tree trunks. We visit market and gaol, where a mad murderer performs for our benefit. Wonderful people the Sudan service. Ingleson served under <u>Eden</u>, & has not seen him since last war.

Tritton collects a couple more Kiwis—he is a born Autolycus.[96]

Wireless tells us that "Clyde" flying boat wrecked by hurricane in Lisbon Harbour. Is this the one that was to take us to England? Does this mean a week in Lagos, on the Slave Coast? Does this mean Yellow Fever and Sweat? Who knows?

Among guests at dinner is one Tom Menzies, from Ayrshire—I must tell Pat!

<u>Monday Feby 17th</u>   Across flat and uninteresting yellow country to MAIDUGURI, to KANO—a great market centre, to LAGOS, the capital of Nigeria—on the delta of the Niger. After Fort Lamy and before Maiduguri, we cross a "grey green greasy river"[97] whose name I must look up. From Cairo to within a couple of hundred miles of Lagos the landscape is dreary, with <u>no</u> signs of the famous African jungle, and few signs of habitation—a great surprise to me. At Kano, see an old Arab city in reasonable preservation.

Along this route, remote a couple of years ago, Hurricanes fly every day on their way to reinforce the Middle East, a most satisfying sight and sound.

Governor of Lagos—Sir Bernard Bourdillon—very good—born at Burnie in Tasmania. Meet at dinner General Hawkins (knows the Fairbairns)[98] and Brigadier Grimley, transferred ironically from Ireland to Lagos! Bourdillon very blunt about Dakar. Nobody's fault but Winston's. Attacking forces were at Freetown for 5 days, so that every element of surprise disappeared. Governor of Gibraltar meanwhile not informed as to whether French cruisers to be stopped or not.[99]

N.B. These colonial governors are frequently very good, and have intimate first hand knowledge. Are they consulted enough?

<u>Tuesday Feb 18th</u>

After a sweltering night, leave Lagos early and fly over green, well-watered, thickly wooded (many palm trees, for palm oil) and occasionally swampy coast to Freetown—a considerable and modern looking town with a

---

96   Autolycus, the son of Hermes and Chione, lived on Mount Parnassus and was renowned as the master-thief of antiquity.

97   'The great grey-green, greasy Limpopo River, all set about with fever-trees' from Rudyard Kipling's 'The Elephant Child' in *Just So Stories* (1902).

98   A Victorian pastoral and political family. James Fairbairn, a close colleague and Minister for Civil Aviation in Menzies' first Cabinet, was killed in a plane crash near Canberra in 1940.

99   A reference to an incident in September 1940 when an Anglo-Free French force attempted to gain control of Dakar, a Vichy French base in North Africa, 'the Gibraltar of the Atlantic', to neutralise French warships based there. The assault was bungled, the element of surprise was lost, and the Vichy French fought back.

fine spacious harbour in which there are at present scores and scores of ships—no doubt awaiting escort.

Reflections Tales of Beaverbrook's high-handedness come drifting in.[100] The history of war is that of one man building on another's foundations. The flashy and the unscrupulous seem to come to the top. The public are very child-like: they like something that rattles. It is the age of publicity, which means that the most illiterate of all trades, that of newspaper writing, becomes dominant. Judgment is handed over to the unjudicial. The man of words is treated as a man of action, provided the words are sufficiently rhetorical to reach the ears of a press reporter. Someone should write a book, or at least an ode, "to the unknown men in war". It all takes me back to the Libyan campaign—Wavell will get a peerage and a place in history, while O'Connor will get a C.B. !

Wednesday Feb 19th

At Bathurst, where we meet Governor Soulton (whose wife knows the Poolmans & the Brookes (Hong Kong) & is some sort of cousin of Tritton,[101] Pilot decides that, after 2 hours refuelling, we can fly through the night to Lisbon—which we do. Quite an experience, passing from tropics to sharp cold at about 1 am. Arrive Lisbon 9 am after record 26 hours flight of 3600 miles! The last hop—Bathurst to Lisbon, is longer than from Ireland to Newfoundland!

Lisbon is in aftermath of a hurricane, in which "Clyde" sunk (we are on "Clare"), Storey losing his papers and perhaps his films, and Landau staying behind as watchdog.

Wireless mast blown down, and so (unknown to us) our pilot comes through without beam and on dead reckoning. Not received by Embassy, and in ill temper accordingly.[102] Lisbon a dull day, but attractive city along the sea. Stay at Palacio Hotel Estoril. Houses of colour, with tiles and wrought iron balconies the chief features. Dine at Embassy. Ambassador Sir Ronald Campbell, who was at Paris during the final days. Minister Sir Noel Charles. Letter for Madrid from

---

100   Lord Beaverbrook (Maxwell Aitken), Canadian-born British newspaper magnate, politician, crony of Churchill and Minister of Aircraft Production. According to Colville, 'many people thought he was evil. He was, in fact, impish and he was capable of great kindness'. *Fringes*, p. 539.

101   Menzies omits closing bracket.

102   Channon, who had travelled with Menzies from Cairo, recounted the arrival in his diary: 'Everywhere else there had been officials and red carpets, but here the Embassy had done nothing, and the Prime Minister of Australia was allowed to land like any ordinary traveller ... Menzies, hungry, unshaven and affronted, was in a rage. I tried to calm him by ringing up the Embassy but there was no reply. At last we got into a car, Menzies and I, and drove to Estoril where no rooms had been reserved. I made a row and procured one which we shared for a few hours ... whilst he bathed I slipped below and rang up Noel Charles ... The Embassy obviously had been caught napping.' *Chips*, p. 292.

Arthur Yencken,[103] who, like many others, speaks in glowing terms of Sam Hoare's work as Ambassador. He has apparently been largely responsible for a complete swing in Spanish opinion.[104]

At dinner at Embassy, Campbell and I have most interesting talk.

1.   Too much talk of "Vichy Govt" an error—these people must be given a discreet backing. Pétain is of good standing with the French, and, after his initial weakness (or innocence accepting an armistice from an honourable foe!) he has done well.

2.   Better we should build up France than Czecho-Slovakia. Latter is of no real moment per se.

3.   Why were the politicians of France so bad? My theory is—no power of dissolution, and so bargain ousted the ballot. This was the end of democracy.

---

103   Arthur F. Yencken, British Minister in Madrid since 1940, had been born and educated in Melbourne.

104   Sir Samuel Hoare, Home Secretary under Chamberlain, had been appointed Ambassador to Spain by Churchill in May 1940 and charged with the difficult task of maintaining Spanish neutrality. Madrid was a great centre of both Allied and enemy activity and Hoare managed to establish excellent relations with the authorities, securing the release from Spanish prisons of some 30 000 Allied prisoners of war and refugees.

20 February – 2 May

Met by Stanley Bruce, the Australian High Commissioner, Menzies is installed in a
suite at the Dorchester Hotel in London, at the outset of what becomes a ten-week
period spent in Britain. Planned to be shorter, the stay is extended twice, despite anxious
warnings from his wife that political plots against him at home require a timely return.
On 20 March Menzies decides to stay an extra fortnight, to follow up successes which
he and Storey are having in obtaining advice and cooperation from British industrial
firms about extending the production of war materials in Australia. Then, on 14 April,
crisis in the Middle East leads him to decide to remain for two more weeks because he
believes that 'grave decisions' are about to be made on the fate of Australian troops
there, and as Prime Minister he should be involved.

 The fortuitous fact that Menzies' visit coincides with Britain's decision to aid
Greece in resisting Nazi aggression gives these weeks for him their central thread of
tension. He attends the meeting of the British War Cabinet which agrees to send
troops—primarily Australian—to Greece; he experiences at close quarters the first days
of watching that hazardous undertaking; he is appalled and angry when what he sees
as a British 'botch' leads to defeat in Greece and the rapid loss of most of what the
victorious Australians, whom he has only just left, had won in Libya. And throughout,
he is needled from home by an uneasy Cabinet and by outspoken critics to whom it is
impossible for him, given the censorship imposed by war, to divulge his real feelings of
strain and indignation. Menzies' changing appreciation of these matters are the
underlying determinants of his relationship with Churchill, the seeming dictator of
British strategy. But, for at least the first third of the visit, he is as much dazzled as
annoyed by Churchill, who for his part considers Menzies, from the beginning, as one
with whom 'it is agreeable to dine'. Altogether he spends six of his weekends at
Chequers, the Prime Minister's official country retreat, and there meets many
interesting ministers and officials, foreign as well as British. There is, however, a steep
decline in Menzies' regard for Churchill in the last two weeks of the visit. The Diary
vividly documents this change: it is a clash of personalities, a reflection of deep anxiety
about Australian troops in Greece, and also of resentment at Churchill's brusque
rejection of a recipe which, in his naiveté, Menzies offers for improved relations with
Eire. He sets this out in a long memorandum for the War Cabinet after making a trip to
Eire and having long talks with de Valera.

 First-hand experience of air raids and observation of their terrible results are, for
a man coming from the peace and remoteness of Australia, a devastating experience.
The Diary captures these feelings well: there is some of the old joy experienced on former
trips to England, but much is dissipated by the stern demands of war: 'old friends,'

Menzies writes, 'are ships that pass in the night.' There are moments of heart-heaviness, when he feels 'very homesick and depressed. London's savour has gone. A city living in darkness is queer, and life becomes formless.' He nevertheless is much in the public eye, as a sought-after speaker, and momentarily feels that the best contribution he can make to the war effort is to help keep up the spirits of the British people, whose courage wins his unbounded admiration. Indeed, there is a hint of wishing that he could stay and find a niche in public life in England.

Thursday 20th

Approaching England, we fly low. There is a tension in the nerves, a feeling of "running the gauntlet". We'll all be happy to arrive. Flying very low—under the clouds. A very unpleasant finale to our voyage. Zig-Zag. We are now travelling, by the sun, S.E.! 250 miles off land, we are picked up by an escort of a Blenheim and a Beaufort; it makes you feel a little better.

Off Mundy Island[1] it begins to snow! And two days ago we were at Lagos. This air travelling requires the constitution of a horse.

Come in across N. Devon. Many fields white with snow. The dark woods, the myriad hedges. What a lovely place at any time.[2] "Land" at Poole, received by Bruce,[3] Bromley[4] (who ask specially about Pat) and a party of press. My teeth chattering with unaccustomed cold, I am forced, in front of the usual English crowd of sight seers, to speak into a microphone for a movie-camera man. We then go to a small inn, where there is a quick press interview, followed by a broadcast interview—the kind of thing I shy at very much, but which got through fairly well. Bruce & I then drive, with dim lights, through a black out country through Winchester & Canterbury to Clive Baillieu's House "Parkwood" now tenanted by a Canadian named Banks—portion being sub-let to Bruce as a country retreat. Along all the dark roads you see troops in ones or twos. When I go to bed, after a very sound dinner (if you grow your own fowls &c rationing does not affect you) I am lulled to sleep by the reasonably distant concussion of guns.

---

1   Menzies presumably means Lundy Island in the Bristol Channel just off North Devon.

2   Channon comments in his diary: 'The excitement of Menzies' Australian entourage was touching to see as they approached England for the first time.' *Chips*, p. 293.

3   Stanley Melbourne Bruce, former Australian Prime Minister, now Australian High Commissioner in London.

4   Rear-Admiral Arthur Bromley, ex-Royal Navy, representing the Dominions Office.

<u>Friday Feby 21st</u> Up to London. Snow still lying. First type of balloon barrage—silvery looking "blimps" a few thousand feet up. Not in rows, but singly or in small groups. Bruce quotes a bright remark of some political wit— "when a balloon is on the ground it looks like Tom Inskip; when it is up in the air it looks like Lord Caldecote!"[5]

So to the Dorchester, where, on the 1st floor, I have the suite which was occupied by Wendell Wilkie.[6] As the building is modern and there are seven floors above me, it is considered as good as an air raid shelter. Curtains are closely drawn at sunset: the windows are coated with some anti-shatter mixture. Day raids have for the time been practically discontinued, and the street traffic on the way to the Dept of Information (London University) and Australia House seemed almost normal. So far I have seen only a few bombed places, including the house in Piccadilly where the Duke of York lived. Sandbags everywhere; barbed wire; the front (to the Mall) of Carlton House Terrace rather battered; King Charles at Charing Cross in a corrugated iron container; police in tin hats; not many people carrying their gas masks; AIR RAID SHELTER, or AIR RAID TRENCHES signs everywhere; windows bricked or boarded up. At Information Dept I have a guard of Honour of the Home Guard (who work in offices and do their stuff as guards so many nights a week!) and some Australians still left here. In a large room find I have to address about 200 international press, under the glare of Kleig lamps & the rattle of cameras. Duff Cooper & Walter Monckton K.C. (now Director)[7] on the platform. Questions put and answered. They say afterwards that I did well and press reaction should be good.[8]

At Australia House, meet the whole staff and thank them for prompt and devoted work. This timely and much appreciated.

Lunch with Bruce at Savoy. Dalton,[9] H. Morrison,[10] Bevin,[11] Lord

---

5   Lord Caldecote, the Lord Chief Justice, was Thomas W.H. Inskip before his elevation to the peerage.

6   Wendell Willkie, Republican candidate for the 1940 US Presidential election, had visited London in January 1941 as President Roosevelt's goodwill envoy.

7   Alfred Duff Cooper, Minister of Information. Sir Walter Monckton, Director-General, and head of Cooper's staff.

8   Menzies told the British press: 'Australians are fighting with you because they are great-grandsons of people who were your great-grandfathers. We are a family ... The people of Britain, even in the darkest hour of trial, must never believe they are standing alone.' *Sydney Morning Herald*, 22 February 1941.

9   Hugh Dalton, economist and Labour MP, was Minister of Economic Warfare. Dalton found Menzies 'very hearty, amusing and intelligent'. They had first met in Melbourne in 1938, when Menzies had said to him: 'I am delighted and astonished to meet a member of the British Labour Party who has a sense of humour,' and he had replied, 'I am equally delighted and astonished to meet an Australian Conservative who has some intelligence.' *Dalton*, p. 163.

10   Herbert Morrison, a Labour MP, was Home Secretary and Minister of Home Security.

11   Ernest Bevin, trade union leader and Minister of Labour and National Service, was a member of the War Cabinet.

Woolton,[12] Hankey,[13] John Anderson,[14] Lyttelton.[15] Very easy and informal, and if there was any ice to break I did not notice it.

Bruce thinks Woolton good, but as he is quiet and perhaps a little deaf I could not get a clear impression. He is the pure business man. Bevin is rotund, cheerful and self-confident, with an occasional dropped H. Plainly would be a great hand with a fractious union, but I would think of limited mental powers. Herbert Morrison lacks one eye, but is rather arresting; smallish, humorous, broadminded, I feel I must get to know him, and I had an instinctive feeling that we would get on. Will be surprised if Lyttelton is of real tonnage.

Very free talk about Southern Ireland. All present are plainly anti-R.C. Bevin convinced that some Federal Scheme the only way out (probably right!) and that now is the time for a commission from the dominions, chaired by U.S.A. to offer to settle the matter!

Dine quietly at Dorchester with my party & Alfred Stirling,[16] who is thinner but in good form. Tomorrow to "Chequers" for a weekend with Winston.[17]

Saturday Feb 22nd

Did not sleep very well. This thick curtaining of windows and closing of the windows themselves induces a sort of claustrophobia which is so far irritating to the nerves. It has other defects, e.g. if the sitting room has been smoked in, there is no way of airing it until the morning, when the smell is terrific. However, one must not complain.

This morning's papers good—excellent report in "Times" and leader in "Telegraph". After lunch run up to see the Temple, where devastation very bad,

---

12   Lord Woolton (Frederick James Marquis), a businessman who had become Minister of Food under Chamberlain and acquired a national reputation as an administrator.

13   Lord Hankey, long the powerful Secretary to the British Cabinet and to the Committee of Imperial Defence. Chamberlain had made him a peer and brought him into the Cabinet; Churchill kept him on, but demoted him, as he remained a loyal—and potentially dangerous—Chamberlainite.

14   Sir John Anderson, Lord President of the Council and Independent MP. In 1938, as Lord Privy Seal with special responsibility for civil defence, he had commissioned the design of the outdoor household air raid shelters, popularly known as 'Anderson shelters', which proliferated from 1939.

15   Oliver Lyttelton, President of the Board of Trade.

16   Alfred T. Stirling, Australian External Affairs Officer in London, had been Menzies' private secretary when he was Attorney-General, and they had maintained a close correspondence ever since in which they discussed travel, literature and the theatre as well as politics.

17   'Chequers', the official country home of British prime ministers, situated near Wendover in Buckinghamshire, 30 miles (50 km) north-west of London. It was the gift of Viscount Lee of Fareham who in 1917, with parliamentary approval, set up the house as a weekend retreat and place for prime ministers to entertain guests.

City, and Gray's Inn. The genius with which these Germans have happened upon ancient landmarks with their bombs is terrible. Once you get past St Paul's, you come on whole blocks of which only an occasional twisted girder or brick wall remains. At Gray's Inn, no structural damage except in dessert room and library, but pitted everywhere. Impressions. It will still take a long time to wipe out London. The police and fire fighters are superb. Curious to see important memorials (e.g. at Hyde Park Corner) bricked up for the war.

In evening, with snow falling across the purplish smudges of the Chiltern Woods, to Chequers for the week-end. The entrance drive and circle have been grassed over; they were too much of a landmark from the air. The house is closely guarded, with sentries in every direction.

In the Long Gallery (much more lived in and attractive) I meet Mrs Churchill who is in good form (but irritates Winston a little, as no doubt most people do), Mrs Randolph Churchill, very pretty with red brown hair and a new baby, and Mary Churchill, aged 17, the freshest and best looking girl I have seen for years. Lord Cranborne[18] & wife also present. Winston "enters" wearing what is called a Siren Suit, a dull blue woollen overall, with a zipp fastener up the front. "As worn", I believe, for the sudden alarm and retreat to the basement. As a form of pre-prandial costume it mystified me, for he later appeared at dinner in the white shirt of convention, and forgot all about air raids until 2 a.m.![19]

Cranborne is an earnest light weight whose fidelity to Anthony Eden has gained him advancement. I cannot see him ever putting a matter up hard to Cabinet, and vis à vis Winston his policy plainly is to say Yes. Well, perhaps that is too severe, for if the evening's conversation is any criterion the P.M. would not actually hear anybody who said No. What a tempestuous creature he is; pacing up and down the room, always as if about to dart out of it, and then suddenly returning. Oratorical even in conversation. The master of the mordant phrase and yet, I would think, almost without real humour. Enjoys hatred, and got a good deal of simple pleasure out of saying what he thought of DeValera,[20] who is (inter alia) a murderer & perjurer. [N.B. There is a growing passion on this subject here, and we may as well get ready for squalls. After all, why should the British people, (and the Australian) be prejudiced and perhaps defeated by this fantastic Southern Irish neutrality?] Winston awaits American action after the

---

18 Lord Cranborne (R.A.J. Gascoyne-Cecil), Secretary of State for Dominion Affairs.

19 Menzies was not the only person to be taken aback by the famous siren suit. Channon relates a story that Lord Halifax had seemed so surprised by it that Churchill had explained, 'Clemmie bought me these rompers!' *Chips*, p. 277.

20 Eamon de Valera, Prime Minister of the Republic of Eire. Menzies is not sure of the spelling of 'de Valera' and has various versions.

passing of the "lease and lend" bill,[21] but I endeavoured vainly to get his mind on the question of the ultimate solution of Ireland. War? Federal Union? Should the Dominions offer to intervene?[22]

Winston is completely certain of America's full help, of her participation in a Japanese war, and of Roosevelt's passionate determination to stamp out the Nazi menace from the earth. Is he right? I cannot say. If the P.M. were a better listener and less disposed to dispense with all expert or local opinion, I might feel a little easier about it. But there's no doubt about it; he's a holy terror—I went to bed tired!

Sunday Feb 23rd

Study cables &c in bed and also "Sunday Times" where my friend Atticus describes me (horribile dictu) as "a great genial, back-slapping Melbourne barrister". Then a walk with the family across the snow, down to Great Kemble[23]—a lovely walk through the winter woods.

At lunch, General Macfarlane, late 2nd in C/d Gibraltar, impresses me very much. Net result—The heaviest I Tanks and Bren gun carriers—the cruiser no use—he makes the worst of both worlds.

Afternoon visit Control Room of fighter squadrons near Uxbridge—60 feet underground and a miracle of efficiency co-ordinating squadrons & AA guns over a Command covering the vital S.E. of England. Return to make broadcast and then visit Carl Winter at Wendover. Carl quite changed—correct, official, thinner & older, & almost academic.[24]

At night we have Bomber Command (Sir Richard Pearse)[25] and Fighter Command (Sir Sholto Douglas) for dinner. Momentous discussion later with P.M. about defence of Greece, largely with Australian & New Zealand troops. This kind of decision, which may mean thousands of lives, is not easy. Why does a peaceable man become a Prime Minister?[26]

---

21   In June 1940 President Roosevelt had committed the United States to aiding materially 'the opponents of fascism'. But under existing US law Britain and other Allies had to pay for purchases of war materials such as military equipment, food and raw materials in cash. By December 1940 Churchill had warned Roosevelt that Britain could not continue to make these cash payments. In response, Roosevelt proposed to Congress the 'Lend-Lease' bill, whereby he would be empowered to sell, lease or lend articles to the government of any country whose defence he thought vital to the security of the United States in return for payment in kind or other benefit.

22   See Appendix II 'The Trip to Ireland'.

23   Great Kimble.

24   Carl Winter, Keeper of Engravings, Illustrations, etc. at the Victoria and Albert Museum, was the son of Carl Winter and Ethel Hardy of Melbourne.

25   Air Marshal Sir Richard Peirse.

26   See Appendix I 'The Greek Campaign'.

Monday 24th Feb

Lunch with Bruce at Claridge's. Meet some old friends—Lord Riverdale,[27] who gives me a letter from Clare Sydney Smith, de la Warr,[28] Glendyne,[29] Swinton,[30] Malcolm McDonald, McGowan,[31] Harry McGeagh,[32] &c.

In afternoon, discuss the Greek adventure with Bruce & Shedden. S and I both favour scheme with some misgiving—Bruce is more doubtful.

At 5 pm attend War Cabinet at Downing Street. It is decided to proceed subject of course to consent of Aust. Cabinet to use of Australian troops. Nett view, the project has some reasonable chance of success; if it fails (says Winston) personnel can be got off; it is our only hope of influencing Turkey & Yugo-Slavia. We cannot afford to leave Greece in the lurch. Above all, American opinion will respond.

Whole matter was discussed in three quarters of an hour, and would have finished in ten minutes but for some queries raised by me regarding air support, problems of equipment, of shipping and of time.[33]

Procedure interesting. Chiefs and Assistant Chiefs present, also P.U.S. for Foreign Affairs, & Sir Alec Cadogan[34] & a few others. Winston—plus cigar says

---

27   Lord Riverdale (Arthur Balfour), industrialist and government adviser.

28   Lord De la Warr (Herbrand 'Buck' Sackville), First Commissioner, Office of Works and Public Buildings.

29   Lord Glendyne (John Nivison), of the stockbroking firm Nivison and Co. which handled Australian loans in London. Menzies later stays at Glendyne's country estate, 'Herontye', in Sussex.

30   Lord Swinton (Philip Cunliffe-Lister), who as Chamberlain's Air Minister had made decisions (ordering Spitfires and Hurricanes on prototype evidence, dramatically increasing pilot recruitment and training, and fostering research on radar) which proved crucial to Britain's subsequent survival in the war.

31   Sir Harry Duncan McGowan, Chairman of Imperial Chemical Industries Ltd since 1930.

32   Colonel Sir Henry Foster MacGeagh, Judge Advocate-General, Army and Air Force since 1934.

33   As a matter of courtesy, Menzies was admitted to the British War Cabinet during his time in London. Cabinet minutes indeed record him on this date asking difficult questions, which culminated in the following exchange: 'MR MENZIES said that ... if the enterprise was only a forlorn hope, it had better not be undertaken. Could he say to his colleagues in Australia that the venture had a substantial chance of success? THE PRIME MINISTER [Churchill] said that in the last resort this was a question which the Australian Cabinet must assess for themselves on Mr Menzies' advice. In his (the Prime Minister's) opinion, the enterprise was a risk which we must undertake. At the worst he thought that the bulk of the men could be got back to Egypt, where new equipment could by then be provided.' War Cabinet Minutes, 24 February 1941, PRO CAB 65/21/26.

34   Sir Alexander Cadogan, Permanent Under-Secretary of State for Foreign Affairs. His diaries, published after his death (David Dilks (ed), *The Diaries of Sir Alexander Cadogan O.M. 1938–1945*, London, 1971), revealed an extraordinary and unsuspected streak of vituperative contempt for politicians.

"First Sea Lord", and Pound[35] speaks regarding losses & events—very clearly & crisply. A few questions, chiefly by P.M. Same with others. Then Greek affair called on. "You have read your file, gentlemen, report of the Chiefs of Staff C'tee. The arguments are clear on each side. I favour the project". And then around the table. Nobody more than three or four sentences. Does this denote great clarity and directness of mind in <u>all</u> these Ministers, or has Winston taken <u>charge</u> of them, as the one man whom the public regard as indispensable! There may be a good deal in this business of <u>building yourself up</u> with the public by base arts so that you can really control a Cabinet.[36]

<u>People.</u> Tentative Estimate.

Herbert Morrison—Yes

Cranborne—Courtesy has ousted fibre

Anderson will not cross Churchill

Alexander[37] disagrees in silence and tells you privately next day

Beaverbrook has a mind of his own, though I suspect it is not a good mind

Sinclair[38] (Air) light as air

Greenwood[39] present, & hopes to be correct

Attlee[40] should be a Sunday School Superintendent

Atmosphere—marvellous people at creating it—I was the only one to put questions, and feel like a new boy who, in the first week of school, commits the solecism of speaking to the captain of the School.

For dinner and the night to Windsor—per black-out—a weird experience. As night falls a few stragglers hurry home, and the footpaths become empty and echoing. Dine, à trois, with King & Queen. He shows no trace of stammer & speaks often loudly with a kind of excitement. She looks older but as fascinating as ever. McKenzie King is behind scratch.[41] Very friendly & informal. Undercurrent—Edward VIII should not have abdicated, and damaged cause of peace by doing so when he did.

<u>Tuesday 25th Feb</u> Take picture of Royal Family in court yard. Young princesses much smaller and shyer than I expected, but natural. After King

---

35 Admiral Sir Dudley Pound, First Sea Lord.

36 See Appendix III 'Appraising Churchill'.

37 Albert Victor Alexander, First Lord of the Admiralty.

38 Sir Archibald Sinclair, Leader of the Liberal Party from 1935 and Secretary of State for Air since 1940.

39 Arthur Greenwood, Deputy Leader of the Labour Party, appointed Minister without Portfolio but in January 1941 charged with the study of reconstruction and postwar problems.

40 Clement Richard Attlee, Leader of the Labour Party and Lord Privy Seal.

41 W.L. Mackenzie King, the Canadian Prime Minister, is apparently being criticised by the Queen.

departs, Queen takes me into her room and we have an hour. She is as wise as possible, and has the shrewdest estimate of all the Cabinet, including Winston, whose weakness for Yes-men she regrets (Later today Duke of Kent said "He has 6 ideas a day; they can't all be right!")

At lunch I meet (new) Balfour,[42] who looks very good, Alexander, Margesson (good)[43] and Butler (query).[44]

After cabling Australia re Greece,[45] see Duke of Kent & dine with Victor Cazalet[46] at Dorchester. Call on Oliver Stanley[47] (ill with a cold).

Wednesday 26th Feb

General talk with Dutch Minister & Foreign Minister who talk of going to Australia.

Lunch at Dorchester—National Defence Public Interest Committee. Lord Nathan of Churt in Chair ("The Nathan action").[48] Present 700 including Athene Seyler,[49] Nicholas Hannen,[50] Irene & Violet Vanbrugh,[51] all of whom very pleasant. Also Nuffield,[52] no fool, who is profane, friendly, & delivers me from a few bores. Impression grows that best value of this mission is to encourage and lift up the people here. They have had a bad time and want a boost to their spirits. Bruce pleased, but as usual undemonstrative. Hugh McIntosh[53] present, and delighted.

Afterwards to F.O., where Butler and Cadogan fail to prove that they know more than we do. Frankly, drift seems policy of F.O. but I hope that

---

42	Captain Harold Balfour, Conservative MP and Parliamentary Under-Secretary for Air.
43	Captain David Margesson, Secretary of State for War.
44	Major Richard Austen Butler ('RAB'), Parliamentary Under-Secretary of State for Foreign Affairs.
45	Menzies to Fadden, 25 February 1941, *DAFP*, vol. IV, pp. 452–3.
46	Major Victor Cazalet, a Conservative MP who had supported Churchill in the pre-war struggle for re-armament.
47	Oliver Stanley, Conservative MP who had been Secretary of State for War under Chamberlain. When Churchill became Prime Minister he had appointed Anthony Eden Secretary of State for War and Stanley rejoined the army in the Future Operations Planning Branch.
48	Lord Nathan, a Labour MP who built up the Army Welfare Service. At the 1935 election Nathan stood unsuccessfully for South Cardiff, his failure in part due to a libel published by the *Western Mail* on the morning of the election and for which the paper subsequently made a public apology in court and paid Nathan substantial damages.
49	Athene Seyler, an actor on the London stage and married to Nicholas Hannen.
50	Nicholas Hannen, an actor.
51	Irene and Violet Barnes, sisters and actors, who both adopted the stage name of Vanbrugh.
52	Lord Nuffield (William Richard Morris), industrialist and philanthropist.
53	Hugh Donald McIntosh, an Australian sporting and theatrical entrepreneur, and newspaper proprietor.

Anthony Eden may satisfy me more. Why should we allow an atmosphere of inevitability to drift into our relations with Japan? We need firmness, definition, and friendliness, and they are not impossible.[54]

At night, dine (during AIR RAID WARNING) at Lansdowne Club with Hugh Dalton, V.F. Hall, Leith Ross[55] &c & explain our economic history.[56]

N.B. Dalton & Co hate and distrust Beaverbrook!!!!, also McKenzie King.!

Thursday 27th Feb

Breakfast with Trevor Smith, whose chief criticism is of air raid shelter muddle at an earlier date. Then to Australia House. Bruce very complimentary, and actually says he has been looking for years for a Prime Minister who knew his business and knew why. Hooray!

Lunch with Bruce and met Crookshank (F.S.T.)[57] sandy side-burns and a silk hat; Ronald Cross[58] (pretty good? a clear head anyway), Attlee (amiable, but otherwise a slightly puzzled Sunday School Superintendent) & Moyne (colonies, and a rank novice at politics).[59]

I already weary of the Socialist Ministers. They are so busy abusing the "old gang" for our unreadiness that they have forgotten their own bad old policy of sanctions with Bows & Arrows. God save us from these doctrinaire democrats.

In afternoon, to a meeting with Service Ministers and Chiefs. What does "cutting our losses in the Mediterranean and going to your assistance" mean? Nobody knows. And anyhow, how can you if you have land forces which cannot be deserted? Clear thinking is not predominant here, I can only hope that action and thought are not considered mutually exclusive. Then to War Cabinet, where, after tying up some loose ends of last meeting's momentous decision, smaller matters supervene. As there is no Country Party, the Agriculture Minister

---

54 Cadogan was also unimpressed: 'Had a meeting at 3.30 with R.A.B., Menzies, Bruce and Shedden—mainly about Far East. What irresponsible rubbish these Antipodeans talk!' Dilks, *Diaries of Sir Alexander Cadogan*, pp. 358–9.

55 Sir Frederick William Leith-Ross, Director-General of the Ministry of Economic Warfare.

56 According to Dalton Menzies gave 'a very interesting account of Australian war finance, taxation, rates of interest, Central Bank credit, and all the great expansion of arms manufacture'. *Dalton*, p. 167.

57 Captain Henry Frederick Comfort Crookshank, Financial Secretary to the Treasury since 1939 and Conservative MP since 1924.

58 Ronald Hibbert Cross, Minister of Shipping.

59 It is curious that Menzies should accuse Lord Moyne (Walter Edward Guinness) of being a novice at politics—he had been an MP since 1907, had been sworn a member of the Privy Council in 1923, and was Minister for Agriculture and Fisheries from 1925 to 1929. After the defeat of the Conservatives in 1929 he had retired from office and devoted much of his time to travel, but on the formation of the Churchill Government he had returned and was now Secretary of State for the Colonies and Leader of the House of Lords.

(Hudson)'s[60] objections to further daylight saving are overruled. Another convoy beaten up. The shipping strain is enormous, and represents our only real chance of defeat.[61] Cross is to let me have a full statement of the shipping facts tomorrow, but there can be no doubt that Australia's export trade is going to suffer.

Friday 28th Feb

New Black-out features keep directing attention to themselves. There are plays and revues and films running, but the performances are confined to the day. You cannot take a stroll either before or after dinner, because the black-out renders it utterly impossible if there is the least cloud (as there has been since I arrived). At each doorway you see a little bag of sand for the proper treatment of incendiary bombs. As there is no "blitz" on, a new psychology is springing up— "I stay in bed. If the bomb's meant for me it'll hit me; if it isn't OK". I have a touch of it myself. But would it survive one real live bomb landing even 200 yards away, in Hyde Park? Australia House quite early becomes a gloomy cavern, out of which you are ushered by the fitful gleam of a hurricane lamp.

Breakfast with Arthur Coles,[62] and arrange with him to do some work for me, as he is here, on ARP[63] and shipping. I will be interested to see how he shapes; his faults may turn out to be superficial.

Then to Kingsley Wood[64] at the Exchequer, where, underneath the cherubic countenance and "bobbishness" of the Chancellor I seem to hear the faint echoes of departmental officials saying "Australia must cut her imports— petrol, newsprint &c more. She cannot indefinitely take more out of the dollar pool than she puts into it". Kingsley Wood promised to let me have all the facts about what they are doing here; I informing him that any differences between us are of degree and not of policy.

Then a special interview (in which I was the attentive listener) with Hannen Swaffer—Daily Herald—long lank dark greasy hair, cigarette ash, a black

---

60 Robert Spear Hudson, Minister for Agriculture and Fisheries.

61 The War Cabinet Minutes for this date note heavy losses in an outward bound convoy: four vessels sunk for certain and nine others either sunk or badly damaged. Menzies also tells Cabinet that while his colleagues in Australia have now agreed to the use of the AIF in Greece they have asked difficult questions about equipment and shipping if withdrawal becomes necessary. 27 February 1941, PRO CAB 65/17/77 and CAB 65/21/32.

62 Arthur Coles, Lord Mayor of Melbourne, 1938–40, businessman and Independent member for Henty in the House of Representatives since October 1940. He was visiting England at his own expense and had intimated his willingness to help Menzies' work there.

63 Air Raid Precautions.

64 Sir Howard Kingsley Wood, Chancellor of the Exchequer, was widely regarded as an amiable and agreeable personality but also as one who could be relied upon to take and maintain the necessary decisions.

coat, but a pretty sound knowledge of the men of the moment and indeed of the last 25 years.[65]

Lunch Gray's Inn—Malcolm Hilbery[66] Treasurer this year—a warm reception. These men, some of whom approach the sere and yellow leaf, have been having a bad time. Apart from the dreadful loss of life, it is hard to see mangled or destroyed things of ancient beauty which you have grown up to love.

To Austin Reed's[67] for some socks. The papers today had a photograph of Winston & myself. Quick perception here; the autograph books were produced in two minutes.

The Douglas's (Irvine and Winnie the Pooh)[68] dined with me at Dorchester; they both look very well indeed.

Saturday March 1st

Saw Willingdons[69] just returned from South America. He looks pale and frail, but she is as noisy and demonstrative as ever. Then to "Chequers" for another week end. Drive down with another daughter—Mrs Duncan Sandys— not quite as pretty because eyes protrude too much; but, like all Churchills, immensely voluble, shrewd, well-informed, and intelligent. This is really the most amazing family. They all admire each other, and a visitor can easily get by if his manners are inconspicuous and his capacity for intelligent listening reasonable. The P.M. in a conversation will steep himself (and you) in gloom on some grim aspect of the war [e.g. tonight shipping losses by Fokker wolf planes[70] and U.boats—the supreme menace of the war, on which, with Dudley Pound, 1st Sea Lord, we have had much talk], only to proceed to "fight his way out" until he is pacing the floor with the light of battle in his eyes. In every conversation he ultimately reaches a point where he positively enjoys the war. "Bliss in that age it was to be alive".[71]

---

65 Hannen Swaffer, journalist, socialist and drama critic, had earlier written of Menzies: 'He is London's latest lion.' From *People*, reported in the *Argus*, 24 February 1941.

66 Sir Malcolm Hilbery, King's Bench Judge.

67 A British chain of menswear stores.

68 Ronald Irvine Douglas, a fellow member of Menzies' well-loved Melbourne Savage Club, had been Lyons' private secretary in 1936–38. He was now manager and editor of Australian Associated Press in London. His wife was called Williamina—'Winnie the Pooh' was her nickname.

69 Lord Willingdon (Freeman Freeman-Thomas) was a former Governor-General of Canada and Viceroy of India. Lord and Lady Willingdon had been Menzies' guests during their visit to Australia *en route* to New Zealand for the centennial celebrations.

70 Focke-Wulf. And see Appendix II 'The Trip to Ireland'.

71 'Bliss was it in that dawn to be alive', William Wordsworth from 'The French Revolution, as it Appeared to Enthusiasts' (1809); also 'the Prelude' (1850), book 9, 1, 108.

Why do people regard a period like this as "years lost out of our lives", when beyond question it is the most interesting period of them? Why do we regard history as of the past, and forget that we are making it?

Sunday March 2nd

A grand walk in a cold wind with young Mary Churchill, who "goes it" uphill at 5 miles an hour, talking all the time and occasionally running after her dog; a marvel (she is, not the dog) of vitality and complete naturalness. Dalton arrives for lunch but plays on muted strings, and is assailed by Winston so violently on the question of Socialism that he makes no come-back whatever.[72]

Professor Lindeman[73] (Oxford—Physics—Alsatian by birth, & naturalised before the last war) is present. Conversational powers not great, but he apparently advises the P.M. on scientific matters and in particular prepares all the graphs which show week by week the progress of the war—the numbers of aircraft, of pilots, of armies, &c., &c.

Beaverbrook's weekly report arrives, and I am delighted to find how really good production is; they estimate now Germany not more than 100 a month ahead of us!

Churchill grows on me. He has an astonishing grasp of detail and, by daily contact with the service headquarters, knows of disposition and establishment quite accurately. But I still fear that (though experience of Supreme Office has clearly improved and steadied him) his real tyrant is the glittering phrase—so attractive to his mind that awkward facts may have to give way. But this is the defect of his quality. Reasoning to a predetermined conclusion is mere advocacy; but it becomes something much better when the conclusion is that you are going to win a war, and that you're damned if anything will stand in your way. Churchill's course is set. There is no defeat in his heart.

Monday March 3rd

At lunch, speak to the Foreign Press Association, which produced a record attendance for the occasion. Subject—The Pacific—a sticky topic, but on

---

72   Hugh Dalton, in his diary, gives a rather different account of the exchanges at lunch, suggesting that Churchill's arguments were 'rather superficial'. Throughout the lunch Menzies, he said, 'sat rather silent, a little over-awed, but he will tell the tale all right in Melbourne when he gets back. P.M. said, "Hitler says that 16 million Jews ought to go and live in Australia. What do you say to that?" He had no good quick answer.' Dalton, p. 169.

73   Professor Frederick Alexander Lindemann, scientific and economic adviser to Churchill throughout the war. Colville notes: 'He had the capacity to explain the most difficult problems in clear, simple, well-expressed English ... He looked with contempt on Jews and coloured people: he was arrogant and impervious to argument when his mind was made up. Yet he was good company when in the mood, never boastful of his achievements, and a loyal friend to Churchill and to many others. He was an acquired taste.' Fringes, p. 544.

a plea for frankness I get by. Policy vis à vis Japan is not appeasement in the sense of offering sops to Cerberus, but a proper blend of friendliness & a plain statement that we can and will defend ourselves and our vital interests.

War Cabinet with P.M. absent (a heavy cold) very like cold soup. I must discover the secret of having my cabinet unwilling to decide any important question in my absence.

Dine with Channon MP at Belgrave Square. R.A. Butler—really intelligent but handicapped by a most colourless voice and manner. Harold Balfour, who impresses me as alert, reasoning, well-informed, and above all conscious of our point of view on the Empire Air Training Scheme J. Llewellin,[74] N° 2 to Beaverbrook—grown pompous since I saw him last, loyal to Beaverbrook (as his friends unquestionably are) but inaccurate as to the facts and correspondingly positive in the expression. Diana Duff Cooper, faded but elegant and sophisticated.[75] "Shakes" Morrison calls in—most attractive but has for some reason "missed the bus".[76]

Tuesday March 4th

A few minutes with Windsor Lewis (DSO),[77] Gubby Allen,[78] Plum Warner[79] and Dick Whiskard.[80] Then George Harrap the publisher, who wants me to write a 50 000 word book on England as I see it. I point out the difficulties & embarrassments, but promise to consider.

---

74   Colonel John Jestyn Llewellin, Parliamentary Secretary of Aircraft Production, 1940–41.

75   Lady Diana Cooper, née Lady Diana Manners, daughter of the Duke of Rutland, was the wife of Alfred Duff Cooper, and a celebrated London beauty.

76   Channon describes the evening in his diary: 'My dinner for the Prime Minister of Australia. Mr Menzies arrived on time and my dinner party was a huge success from the very start, one of the gayest and most riotous festivals I have ever arranged. There was a round table; too little to eat but much to drink, the three supreme ingredients of gaiety. Menzies told lengthy stories with great gusto and imitated me in the Mousky [the Bazaar] of Cairo, etc. He is immense, a raconteur ... full of sense and charm.' Chips, p. 293. Menzies had met, and greatly admired W.S. ('Shakes') Morrison, then Postmaster-General, later Viscount Dunrossil and a Governor-General of Australia, on previous visits to England. His earlier predictions of a great future for Morrison in British politics had not come to pass.

77   Major James Charles Windsor Lewis, DSO 1941, had been ADC to the Governor-General of Australia from 1938 to 1939.

78   George ('Gubby') Allen, Australian-born English Test cricketer. An amateur and a genuine all-rounder, Allen had toured Australia twice, as Captain in 1936–37.

79   Sir Pelham ('Plum') Warner, outstanding cricketer, author and journalist, had been Deputy-Secretary of the Marylebone Cricket Club since 1939. In 1903–04 he had captained the first official MCC team to Australia and he was joint manager of the controversial 'Bodyline' tour of Australia in 1932–33.

80   Dick Whiskard, possibly a son of Sir Geoffrey Whiskard, British High Commissioner to Australia, 1936–41.

On landing in England, at Poole, Menzies speaks briefly to the British press. (Menzies Papers)

At the Ministry for Information Menzies addresses a gathering of 200 journalists on Australia's war effort. (Menzies Papers)

Clement Attlee, Leader of the Labour Party.
(Menzies Film)

Sir Howard Kingsley Wood, Chancellor of the Exchequer.
(Menzies Film)

The Duke of Kent and Lady Astor. (Menzies Film)

John Winant, US Ambassador in London.
(Menzies Film)

Lord Bledisloe, former Governor-General of New Zealand, with Menzies. (Menzies Film)

Menzies and W.S. 'Shakes' Morrison, Postmaster-General. (Menzies Film)

Anthony Eden, Secretary of State for Foreign Affairs, and General Sir John Dill, Chief of the Imperial General Staff. (Menzies Film)

Menzies, accompanied by helmeted air raid wardens, surveys London from the roof of Australia House. (Menzies Papers)

'Clearing up the ruins' after an air raid on London. This picture was taken from the top of St Paul's Cathedral looking towards the Old Bailey. (Australasian, 26 April 1941)

Menzies inspects the devastation caused by air raids on the City of London. (Menzies Papers)

A demonstration of how to put on a gas mask. (Menzies Papers)

Scene of bombing devastation in Coventry. (Menzies Film)

Old Trafford Cricket Ground showing bomb crater in the foreground. (Menzies Film)

Grounded barrage balloon ('blimp') in central London. (Menzies Film)

Cleaning up debris after a bombing raid on London. (Menzies Film)

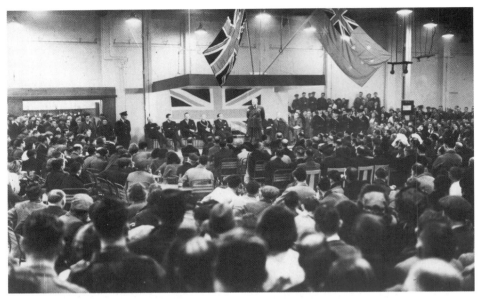

On his visit to Coventry Menzies addresses a large gathering of factory workers in their canteen. (Menzies Papers)

At a parade of London's Civil Defence Services the London Fire Brigade puts on a demonstration for Menzies. (Menzies Papers)

Lunch at Mansion House as guest of L.M., Sir Geo Wilkinson,[81] & speak on bits and pieces. Sit next to Sir Kynaston Studd,[82] and review a little cricket. Outside Mansion House there is a great crater, which it was quicker to bridge than to fill in!

War Cabinet—Winston present. More notes on procedure. P.M. commences with a short but impressive statement on war position. Refers to "battle of the Atlantic". "I expect results, gentlemen". Then a brief expression of faith. Very simple but effective. Discussion very brief. Get through 3 times the work we do. Chiefs of staff do confer. So do Service Ministers.[83] P.M. has direct contact. Individual ministers primarily concerned with own departments. Bevin good, but some conservatives nervous about him. He has more force than Herbert Morrison, but perhaps less character, and a coarser fibre. John Anderson very solid.

Dine with Attlee and Labour Ministers. Very interesting talk about Labour in Australia. Real answer—Irish. They all agree. Attlee, at close quarters, earnest, upright and intelligent. Labour party must have a theory to succeed. Importance of trained men in civil service. Folly of Australian Labour in resisting university graduates. My own philosophy.

1.   When capital is "enterprise capital" (Attlee's phrase), preserve but guide and control private enterprise, which has a dynamic quality.

2.   Otherwise, the State, provided the limits of policy are recognised and properly paid experts attend to general & particular administration.

3.   Socialism cannot succeed on a doctrine of "bread and circuses", but depends ultimately on a spiritual revolution—a new conception of one's duty to the State. A grand evening, David Grenfell[84] excellent. Alexander is sound, but not orthodox Labour. Greenwood "n'existe point".

N.B. What a versatile genius Winston is. At N° 10 Annexe his secretary shows me a series of oil paintings by Winston—one or two really brilliant!!

Wednesday March 5th

One hour to spare, so walkabout for fresh air. Holborn Gray's Inn Road, Theobolds Road, Red Lion Square, Lincoln's Inn Fields—looking lovely in a cold blue grey mist with just a touch of sunlight. Every here and there a few houses destroyed; a shop blown up. We talk of spirit—(each of everybody else's spirit!), but what tragedies of lost or ruined lives must be behind these scattered

---

81   The Lord Mayor of London, Sir George Wilkinson.

82   Sir Kynaston Studd, a former Lord Mayor of London, philanthropist and cricketer, had been President of the MCC since 1930.

83   See Appendix III 'Appraising Churchill' on Churchill as a war leader.

84   David Grenfell, Labour MP and a former miner, became Minister for Mines in 1940.

bricks. It is a bedlamite world, and the hardest thing in it is to discuss and decide (as we do in War Cabinet) policies which, even if successful, must bring the angel of death into many homes. In public affairs at this time the successful leader is he who ignores the individual and thinks and acts in broad terms.

Curious interview with British & Australian press. Some noodle thinks my speech about the Pacific was "appeasement".[85] What a perversion. What a tyranny over inferior minds words and phrases exercise! I must be careful not to say "Good day" to my neighbour. Our true policy vis à vis Japan is firmness & friendliness: the two are not inconsistent.

Lunch & conference with Sir A. Sinclair and his Air off siders. Very useful. On this side we shall get results. Storey very pleased with designing capacity here, and with construction effort generally. Singapore being heavily reinforced with fighters.

War Cabinet. The Middle East proposal is going bad. Why the devil should Eden purport to commit us on facts which he must know are most disturbing and which have an Empire significance?

Dine as guest of Newspaper Proprietors Ass[n], with young Rothermere (Esmond Harmsworth)[86] in the Chair, a good show. Speak on Australia's war effort &c &c and great applause. Then Robertson, Beaverbrook's deputy, demands an account of Libya, and I give it. Rothermere promptly & publicly offers me a post as Special Correspondent if ever I leave politics. Generally, I think much good done. Australia is ace high.

Then, at 11.45 pm, to War Room, for further discussion re Middle East. I like Sinclair.

Germany has swallowed Bulgaria—Psalm 28–3 "Draw me not away with the wicked, and with the workers of iniquity, which speak peace to their neighbours, but mischief is in their hearts".

Thursday March 6th

At film office, see Middle East films, which prove that I am a couple of stone overweight, and a talkie of my Ministry of Information speech, which is very good, simply because I did not know it was being taken.

See Glibank (Ld)[87] who buzzes about an Imperial War Council of Cabinet in a good-natured way, but has an inadequate conception of the difficulties, eg Canada.

---

85   Menzies' speech on the previous Monday, 3 March, was delivered to the Foreign Press Association. The Melbourne *Argus*, 5 March 1941, announced under a headline 'A Maladroit Utterance' that 'Mr Menzies' speech was pure appeasement'.

86   Lord Rothermere, proprietor of the *Daily Mail* and Chairman of the Associated Newspapers group. He and Lord Beaverbrook were the two leading and rival owners of the British mass-circulation press.

87   Handwriting unclear.

Lunch with Empire press correspondents; nothing serious; pleasant foolery and a speech.

Afternoon, confer with Supply Dept—Sir Andrew Duncan[88] very good, with some keen men. Good information acquired regarding what we can produce for Great Britain.

War Cabinet, at which I have to speak plain words about consulting Dominions before grave decisions made affecting them.

Dine with Beaverbrook, who calls on me to describe Libya. About 20 M'sP, plus David Low the cartoonist. Beaverbrook & others very pleased. "A prophet is never without honour save in his own country and among his own people". I think B is friendly, and a later talk with Storey makes me think we may get some result on the aircraft production side.

Friday March 7th

Conference M.A.P.[89] with Beaverbrook and his harried minions. A diverting comedy of bell-pushing, a loud harsh voice, abrupt orders for men and papers. B. is a superb, even if obvious, showman. However, the results of aircraft production are good, though I suspect Philip Swinton laid the foundations.

Give lunch to the Agents-General, who, being largely unemployed and "out of it", were delighted to be recognised.

Called on by de Gaulle[90] regarding New Caledonia & Tahiti. He is very tall, with sad features—a heavy nose and a weakish chin; but I think a good mouth. The reverse of the small, voluble Frenchman of fiction or the music hall stage.

Another conference at N° 10—Smuts[91] has sent in a good cable about the Middle East, which impresses me a lot.

Then to Press Club—the usual—and out with Margaret Gilruth to London, Fire Brigade Hqrs, to Shoreditch, St Thomas's Hospital, and Bermondsey, to a casualty station at Unilever House. Clearest impression—St Thomas's—used to be 700 beds—now 70 in the basement. Four separate times hit by 2000 lb bomb—only 9 people killed! Matron (Hillyers) a bright-eyed elderly woman with the Florence Nightingale cap—like a white lace aspidistra growing out of the top of the head! It is wonderful how these people stick around on what has become a most dangerous duty.

---

88 Sir Andrew Duncan, Minister of Supply, a businessman and former Chairman of the British Iron and Steel Federation and of the Central Electricity Board.

89 Ministry of Aircraft Production.

90 General Charles de Gaulle, recognised by the British Government as leader of the Free French.

91 Lieutenant-General Jan Christiaan Smuts, Prime Minister of South Africa.

Saturday March 8th

To the Admiralty, where A.V. Alexander certainly impresses as knowing his department thoroughly. I emphasise the uselessness of rhetorical phrases such as "cutting our losses in the Mediterranean and proceeding to your assistance". A.V. agrees. They are to give me a realistic statement of

(a) What ships can come East in the near future

(b) What ships could come East if war with Japan broke out.

The real truth, which we are all beginning to see, is that <u>air</u> reinforcement to Singapore and the Far East is the great deterrent (apart from USA) to Japan. The Jap is reported here a poor airman. Even on the naval side, the Second Sea Lord (Phillips)[92] said British fleet would be happy to attack with only 60% of the Japanese force! The Japanese experience in China seems to point to a similar state of affairs in the Army!

Lunch at Simpson's. No beef, no saddle of mutton—it is not an economical joint. Food rationing here is going to bite deep before long.

Away to Chequers again—others present—de Gaulle, Gen Spiers,[93] liaison with French forces for many years—Duncan Sandys.[94] Latter is whole-hogger (hang Hitler and wipe out 40 millions of Germans) but certainly stands up to Winston. But Winston has a superb answer—

"In war—fury

In defeat—defiance

In victory—magnanimity

In peace—good will"

And again, in that manner he has of dredging up modern saws and ancient instances, he reminds us of the Greek story of the conquered who were spared—"These men were spared, not because they were men, but because of the nature of man".[95]

Roosevelt was recently asked about the terms of peace. Wiser man than Woodrow Wilson, he replied—"Peace terms? But the Nazis have not yet been defeated!" There can this time be none of this cant of "peace without victory"; because without victory there can never be peace again in my time.

---

92   Rear-Admiral Sir Tom Phillips, Vice-Chief of the Naval Staff.

93   Major-General Edward Louis Spears. In 1918 he changed his name from Spiers to Spears. Major-General Spears was bilingual in French and English and had been sent by Churchill in 1940 as his special representative with the French Prime Minister.

94   Captain Edwin Duncan Sandys, Conservative MP and son-in-law of Churchill.

95   Colville, recounting the evening in his diary, noted that Menzies had been impressed by Churchill's Athenian story. 'Mr Menzies,' he said, 'contributed to the discussion by a slightly irrelevant, though amusing, account of the way in which an insect called the Cactoblastus, imported from California, destroyed the dense growth of Prickly Pear jungle in Australia.' *Fringes*, p. 433.

Later, Winston & de Gaulle argue about North Africa—the German infiltration to Casablanca &c. Winston in a siren suit, speaking French "with attack", a good vocabulary, a fairly loud voice, and a total disregard for the rules of syntax. In a lesser man it would be funny! But in this man it is a perfect expression of character. And incidentally de Gaulle understands him! They tell me that Birkenhead[96] used to say that Winston was the only man whose French he understood, and that as the French also understood him there was satisfaction all round.

P.M. explains & defends Dakar; but I am still left clear that the ambiguity of policy which left Gibraltar without instructions re French cruisers meant that Dakar was really defended. The later naval bombardment was not co-ordinated with any plan for landing, and the whole thing was a sad fiasco.

Sunday March 9th

Colonel Donovan calls at Chequers and I have a long talk. This is a good man; easy, composed, comfortable looking, with a good blue eye; an orderly mind and quiet speech. I would readily take his opinion on men or affairs. He has been over to de Valera, and thinks that the core of the problem is the pressure of the R.C. minority in Ulster, led by Cardinal McCrory.[97] Qualifies De Valera's mental honesty by saying that Dev. readily rejects a course of action which may imperil his tenure of office. Thinks D is worried and troubled of conscience for not having made clear to his own people the real moral issues of the war. Donovan thinks there should be (a) an avenue of personal contact between Dev and Churchill

(b) some encouragement to the local people (Catholics) who think as J.M. Dillon[98] does

(c) Some attempt to get rid of any pinpricks against R.C.'s in the North.

The Irish farmer is beginning to discover that neutrality is not profitable, and altogether there are possibilities. But real trouble is ignorance of Irish people, which leaders have not endeavoured to dispel.

Lunch—General Loch. General Pyle—A.A. gunner men. I put in a word about a shortage of predictors.[99]

After lunch to Denham where we see experiments in defence against dive bombers and low flying aircraft. P.M. with touch of bronchitis stays at home, but

---

96   Churchill's friend, Lord Birkenhead (Frederick Edwin Smith).

97   Cardinal Joseph MacRory, Archbishop of Armagh.

98   James Matthew Dillon, Member of the Dáil and Deputy Leader of the Fine Gael. He opposed Irish neutrality in the war.

99   Predictor—an apparatus for automatically providing tracking information for an anti-aircraft gun from telescopic or radar observations.

on our return it is superb to hear him cross examining and directing the experts. He is a marvellous master of all sorts of war-like detail, but contrary to impression, does not dictate to the experts. But he insists on <u>action</u>. He confesses that he does not understand financial problems, and leaves them to others. He can concentrate his energies. He does not see the press or constituents. He calls conferences, dictates memoranda, I should think writes few letters & certainly no departmental ones!

Last night London has its first real blitz since I arrived, and I missed it. Bombs & incendiaries all round my hotel & the West End generally—Café de Paris, where a bomb came right through into the ballroom. Curzon St incendiaries on roof of N° 10 & so on. There is no pretence of a military objective.

Tonight after dinner at which Sir Alan Brooke[100] present—a showy type & not in either appearance or accent the typical professional soldier, drive to London with Mrs Sandys in an armoured car (!) with a light snow falling and air raid warnings blowing.

N.B. Brooke explained about invasion, Germany must have

(a) fighter cover for bombers, and fighter range does not run N. of Wash

(b) immunity from serious naval attack by heavy vessels ∴ narrow waters

Hence Wash to Plymouth as vulnerable area.

<u>Monday March 10th</u>

Curious to see the North Lodge at Buckingham Palace lying in ruins this morning. Houses shattered in Curzon Street. Germans are poor psychologists. If they had left the West End alone the East Enders might have been persuaded that they alone were bearing the brunt of the war! And Buckingham Palace again! ha ha!

Meeting of War Cabinet in special "fortress" just out of London,[101] at which I give the high-lights of Australia's war effort.[102]

Then to War Office—a desultory but useful discussion, out of which we shall get a new and comprehensive appreciation of the Middle East position.

Have Warner, Gubby Allen, Jim Windsor Lewis, & Christopherson (of MCC)[103] to dinner and much good talk of cricket and the war. Helped to take the mind off these dark and hurrying days in London, where the old pleasure

---

100   General Sir Alan Francis Brooke, Commander-in-Chief of the Home Forces since 1940.

101   Dollis Hill War Room, in the north-western suburbs of London.

102   Cadogan commented: 'Menzies then held forth for 40 mins. on Australian war effort. Very impressive, but no one but an Australian would have done it! However, he didn't do it badly.' Dilks, *Diaries of Sir Alexander Cadogan*, p. 362.

103   Stanley Christopherson, Deputy Chairman of the Midland Bank and President of the MCC, 1939–40.

of being here has gone, your old friends, all busy, are ships that pass in the night, a new spectacle of ruin meets you at every turn, the air raid warning wails every night, and the only comfort is that the purple crocuses are out in the park opposite.

Tuesday March 11th

London is drab and grey. There is a tough and determined spirit, but the colour and gaiety have gone. In squares like Berkeley Square, houses ruined, windows boarded up. The shops everywhere with windows reduced to peep holes. The luncheons reduced to oysters & one course (fish or meat or chicken or eggs or cheese). One feels the hurry and pressure of events. Sandbags in the doorways; ground floor windows bricked up; death around the corner. No more leisurely strolling about the Charing Cross Road book shops or sauntering in Piccadilly. But enough!

Polish Foreign Minister calls on me, and wants to exchange diplomatic representatives. I point out difficulties & made no promises.

Lunch with Ronald Cross—Lord Kemsley (brother Lord Camrose)[104] present, and is pressing "We must not let you leave this country!" Lord knows what journalistic stunt he will be working. Interesting talk on future of Conservative Party. After Winston, what? The Labour men are at their propaganda already—"Bevin or Herbert Morrison". The Conservatives are not thinking of it.

Then to House of Commons where I address EPA[105] on Australia's War Effort. In form, and a remarkable ovation at the finish. Amery[106] in the Chair. Lord Denman[107] looking old fashioned but fit, in the audience. Also Huntingfield.[108] Some of these fellows would not mind my defeat at Canberra if they could get me into the Commons. OMNIS IGNOTUS PRO MAGNIFICO.[109]

Then to Over-seas League reception—Lady Willingdon hostess—many Australians, Canadians, NZ, & S. Africans. Speak on the "real league of nations"

---

104   Lord Kemsley (James Gomer Berry) had joined with his older brother Lord Camrose (William Ewert Berry) in a newspaper partnership which lasted thirty-five years. In 1937 they had divided their businesses; Kemsley becoming Chairman of Allied Newspapers (*Daily Sketch, Sunday Graphic, Sunday Times*, etc.) and Camrose taking the *Daily Telegraph*, the Amalgamated Press and the *Financial Times*.

105   Empire Parliamentary Association.

106   Leopold Amery, Secretary of State for India and for Burma.

107   Lord Denman had been Governor-General of Australia from 1911 until 1914.

108   Lord Huntingfield, Australian-born former member of the House of Commons, had been Governor of Victoria from 1934 until 1939.

109   'Omnis ignotus pro magnifico'—'Every unknown a magnifico'.

and the indestructability of the Spirit of Man as distinct from the works of his hands.[110]

Wednesday March 12th

Away to inspect army matters. Camberley Staff College (Maj. Gen Collins) Sandhurst (next door) where I see superb physical instructors with queer accents, intense manners, and springy feet dealing with half naked cadet officers. Then to Farnborough, to the Tanks. The I Tank, 2 cruisers, and Bren gun carriers. How to load a tank on to a truck. Ride in 3 tanks and get bumped on the head, plus gloriously wet and cold. Then to Brompton Road, to the control room of A.A. guns for London. A miracle of science. The A.A. gun will not fail for want of intelligence and trying. To Hyde Park, to inspect a nest of 3″ A.A., where the predictors interest me. It is still clear that Germany has vastly more numerous A.A. defences than Great Britain has.

Dine at Savoy as guest of Lord Nathan, who produces J.M. Keynes,[111] Sir W. Beveridge,[112] P.J. Noel Baker,[113] Gwylim Lloyd George,[114] General Sir Frederick Pyle (London defences, very good) Lord Trenchard,[115] Sir W. Jowitt S.G.[116] &c &c. Beverly Baxter[117] & Vernon Bartlett.[118] Chas Lidbury.[119]

Speak on economic & munitions effort in Australia. Good reception. Long talk with Keynes (who admires Copland and Giblin),[120] re partnership in

---

110   'Any international lunatic,' he told the League members, 'could smash the work of man's hands, but it took more than that to break down the spirit of man—that was indestructible ... Only when our enemy is forced to learn that will he realise he has lost the war.' *Sydney Morning Herald*, 13 March 1941.

111   John Maynard Keynes, the economist, then in the Treasury acting as adviser to Sir Kingsley Wood, was impressed with Menzies and wrote to the Australian economist Douglas Copland: 'He made a great impression on me ... He speaks extraordinarily well, seems a capable politician and, above all, is on top of his job and serious about what matters.' Keynes to Copland, April 1941, Keynes Papers, Kings' College, London. We are grateful to Mr Selwyn Cornish for drawing our attention to this letter.

112   Sir William Beveridge, social reformer and economist. Under-Secretary in the Ministry of Labour and Master of University College, Oxford.

113   Philip John Noel-Baker, Labour politician.

114   Gwilym Lloyd George, son of the former prime minister David Lloyd George, MP for Pembrokeshire and Parliamentary Secretary to the Ministry of Food.

115   Lord Trenchard, Marshal of the RAF—its founding father, and first Chief of Air Staff.

116   Sir William Jowitt, Solicitor-General.

117   Beverley Baxter, a Canadian who became a Conservative MP in 1935, was the editor of the *Daily Express*.

118   Vernon Bartlett, journalist, broadcaster and Independent Progressive MP.

119   Sir Charles Lidbury, Chief General Manager and a Director of Westminster Bank Ltd.

120   Douglas Berry Copland, Australian economist and Commonwealth economic adviser. Lyndhurst Falkiner Giblin, Australian statistician and economist, and Director of the Commonwealth Bank.

disposal of primary products, e.g. wool, and on the importance of blending war effort with an eye on post war work—e.g. aeroplanes & motor cars in Australia.

The guns roar on the Surrey side, and up North night fighters bring down about 5 bombers. Interesting?

Thursday March 13th

Lunch with Admiral Evans[121] and King Haakon of Norway—good and cheerful English. Then to Northwest to see Tornado, Typhoon (swift as eagles) and Halifax, Manchester & Stirling—so big that Beaufighter would fit under one wing. The Boche has something coming to him. Beaverbrook, with a crushed black hat, a dark blue pull-over, a black suit & goloshes over tan shoes, looks, with his puckish face, like a genial parish priest. Meet & drive with J.G. Winant the new U.S. Ambassador—angular, dark sunken eyes, lantern jaws, a shy, grave and reflective manner. A sort of clean shaven Abe Lincoln. Obvious touch of the Puritan, but clear that violence is all that the Boche will understand.[122]

Dine J.P.L. Thomas,[123] Llewellin, A.W. Coles, Storey & Sir Wilfred Freeman[124] (formerly production man for Air & now deputy CAS—very good).

Friday March 14th

War Cabinet works well. Time Table "Mr So and So to attend at 6.15". Department of Information handles air raid & invasion instructions &c.

Ministry of Shipping. Cross a little disappointing, but he knows he is "on the slide" out of the Government. Put up my ideas on shipbuilding in Australia, and find an audience. Essence is that here there can be no night work in shipyards because of blackout, and there is a further discount for bombing. We could therefore do better in Australia.

Lunch with Lord Simon—who is a conscientious but flat host.

See Oliver Lyttelton re trade. He is clear headed & knowledgeable.

Saturday March 15th

Do a broadcast for America, but as Roosevelt broadcasts at about the same time it will not be noticed.

---

121   Admiral Sir Edward R.G.R. Evans, Royal Australian Navy, had commanded the Australian squadron in 1929. After the German invasion of Norway in 1940 he was sent there to establish liaison with the King.

122   John Gilbert Winant, US Ambassador in London. Colville describes Winant as 'a gentle, dreamy idealist, whom most men and all women loved'. *Fringes*, p. 578.

123   James Purdon Lewes Thomas, Lord Commissioner of the Treasury since 1940.

124   Air Marshal Sir Wilfrid Rhodes Freeman, Vice-Chief of the Air Staff. His outstanding contribution to the expansion of aircraft production had, according to Lord Hives of Rolls-Royce, 'enabled the Battle of Britain to be won'. *Dictionary of National Biography 1951–1960* (London, 1971), p. 378.

Lunch with Savage Club.[125] Bombed out of principal room, but carry on. P.V. Bradshaw (amusing mock broadcast) Mark Hambourg[126] plays marvellously, Malcolm McEachern[127] sings. Others present Dale Collins,[128] Reid Dick,[129] James Agate.[130] I am principal guest, & speak to a marvellous reception—on the arts being an essential part of the civilised life we are struggling to preserve.

Then to Godalming to Australian hospital and nurses, and at nightfall to "Herontye" to the Glendynes, where I find Moira quite lovely and composed and Lady G. practising an almost old-world courtesy!

Sunday March 16th

Sleep in most of morning—first time I have had more than 6 hours sleep since leaving home. Then up. The Glendynes have had narrow escapes—a bomb on front lawn, which blew out windows and blew fragments into the walls & ceiling of dining room as the family sat at table, and another crater on the side lawn. Last night we could hear the German planes passing overhead, and some distant thuds. These moonlight nights are good for it.

At night, car breaks down in East Grinstead & I spend an hour very pleasantly in the Air Raid Wardens' depot. A beastly drive through the fog and blackout to London. Total 3 hours instead of an hour. This black-out driving is horrible, particularly when it is accentuated by fog. Roosevelt made a great speech today—America is at war without knowing it!

Monday March 17th

A stupid driver with no sense of direction drives us to Derby where we see the Rolls Royce works (Sidgraves[131]—Chairman & Hives M. Director). Wonderful sand casting & die-casting. Many women employed on hard work. Music half an hour morning & afternoon. Everyone likes it "except a few old fogies".

Research and development amazing. These people are the best because they look forward. Long talk in offices—Storey & I (a good team, though I say it myself) sell the idea of Australian manufacture. Not in one hit, but

---

125   The Savage Club, formed in 1857 and named after Richard Savage, a shady satirical poet who died in a debtor's prison in 1743, was a bohemian club for authors, actors and artists. Menzies, a devoted member of the Melbourne Savage Club, was made an honorary member of the London Savages.

126   Mark Hambourg, Russian-born pianist and composer.

127   Malcolm McEachern, Australian-born international bass singer and Mr Jetsam of the famous BBC comedy program, 'Flotsam and Jetsam'.

128   Dale Collins, Australian-born author.

129   Sir William Reid Dick, sculptor.

130   James Evershed Agate, author and drama critic.

131   Arthur Frederick Sidgreaves.

begin with crankshaft &c—spare parts—<u>but</u> with the scheme of ultimate full production.

Then to Manchester. Dine as guests of Lord Mayor & Dobson[132] (of Avro Armstrong Siddeley)

Two speeches—one on Australian industry & one on Libya. These people are alert, and our friends.

Tuesday March 18<u>th</u>

To the A.V. Roe assembly works—a magnificent workshop and span—and the testing aerodrome, where we see Manchester Bomber—amazingly easily handled for so vast a machine—the Douglas Reconnaissances, and the rest. Avro-Ansons still produced as trainers. 16 000 employees in all. Test pilot Worrall, whom I identify at once as son of late Rev. Henry Worrall. Managing Director R.H. Dobson—Lancashire. "Mr St<u>oa</u>ry"—"The V<u>u</u>lture Engine &c". Then to main Avro factory, where, at lunchtime, I speak to 9000 cheering employees, and dwell on prospect of depositing 2 tons for 1 of bombs on Germany. A cheerful factory. Lancashire Humour is dry and unbeatable.

In Manchester, as much as 3 blocks adjoining completely destroyed. Say £10 m (but at Sheffield £30 m!)

Visit the wrecked Old Trafford Cricket Ground. Hole in pitch. Stands ruined. Presented with part of an incendiary bomb for M.C.C.

Across Derbyshire mountains with drift snow—lovely country and upland moors, to Sheffield, via Sydney Smith's headquarters. Clare & Sydney well, but tired of a static post looking after balloons.

Stay with Riverdale and dine at Club—"Master Cutler", Lord Mayor &c & am called on to tell the story of Libya again.

This is a valuable and successful journey. So far a quiet night. We seem to miss the actual Blitz by a few days wherever we go. N.B. women used in Air Force—typing, driving, decoding &c. <u>Not</u> to be done unless necessary, because there will be <u>no</u> birthrate hereafter. Many hundreds of women doing quite hard work in factories. Independence and childbirth—will they be thought compatible?

Wednesday March 19<u>th</u>

Sheffield. Visit Moore's works—Micrometers. Miss Halliwell[133] speaks—once factory hand. Old wages book 1910 produced—gift of Sheffield plate—I reply.

---

132   Roy Hardy Dobson, aircraft engineer and Managing Director of Avro Armstrong Siddeley.

133   Marion Halliwell had begun work thirty years earlier as an office girl at Moore's and was now a senior director of the company.

Then Firth's Stainless Steel—& Steel Corporation England. Hydro electric presses gun barrels up to 14″—Battleship plates up to 14″. Sheffield has suffered gravely. 60,000 out of 180,000 houses affected—But industries going magnificently. Spirit superb. No surrender. <u>No</u> compromise.

(Miss Halliwell—"They may bomb our homes and our factories, our bodies. But they can't bomb our skill or our spirit".)

Lunch at Town Hall, when I speak to a representative body, after receiving various gifts, at which Sheffield specialises. Master Cutler Wood explains why "Joseph Rodgers" has faded and "Firth Stainless" has covered a multitude of sins.

Then by lovely country, to Birmingham—Lucas works—cheering crowds—gun turrets for aeroplanes and tanks. 25000 employees! Call on Lord Mayor & see R.E. Priestley,[134] now V.C. Birmingham University.

Then to Himley Hall—Lord Dudley[135]—& Billy Rootes.[136]

Thursday March 20th

Plainly must stay here extra 14 days. There are great possibilities.

Drive to Coventry and meet Mayor & Town Clerk. Inspect ruined city blocks and a destroyed Daimler factory. Also Coventry Cathedral, of which only walls and a fine spire remain. Every where women cheer. They are homely but quick. Australia is popular. At "Council House" Mayor proposes health & I reply.

Then to Rootes factory—new and marvellous. "Daylight lighting" better than I have seen before. Splendid hospital. Medical officer £2000 p.a.!

At vast meeting in Canteen, address thousands of men & women as "brave soldiers of Great Britain". Then lunch & away by Stratford on Avon, Broadway, Gloucester and Cheltenham to Bristol—Stay at house of Sir Stanley White (M-D of Bristol Co). Air raid warnings from London. They study beams from Germany, and where they cross is the place. Loud noises from the city after dinner, but we talk, as usual, until midnight. Billy Rootes with me, Rowbotham, designer of engines for Bristol Co. The young see the problems of British co-operation & salesmanship but the old do not. "We have no plan for salesmanship"—as if that is a final & conclusive judgment.

Speak on 'phone to Mrs Somerville (Whiskard's daughter).

---

134   Raymond Edward Priestley, Antarctic scientist, had been the first Vice-Chancellor of Melbourne University, 1935–38, before returning to England as Vice-Chancellor of Birmingham University in 1938.

135   Lord Dudley, Commissioner for Civil Defence, Midland Region.

136   William Edward Rootes, leading industrialist and government adviser. He and his brother Reginald founded a motor-car manufacturing empire based on the Hillman and Humber factories in Coventry which Menzies visited.

Coventry has lost one third of its rateable value already! But factory production is high. The British have no love for planning, but a genius for improvisation.

At Coventry, call and see birth place of Sir Henry Parkes[137]—quaint old brick cottage.

Friday March 21st

Inspect Bristol works and address, directly in the Canteen or indirectly by loudspeakers, 20 000 employees.

Then through Bristol (with its main shopping streets blitzed—no possible military objective) and by Bridgewater,[138] Taunton, Exeter to Plymouth, which had a doing last night. Many ruins still smoking. Meet Lady Astor[139] at her house on the Hoe. Windows broken, and therefore sent to Admiral's Residence, after visiting a shelter for homeless & speaking there.

At dinner we are warned that Hun arrives two nights running. Sure enough, just as the port arrives we are hurried into the cellars, into a corridor whose floor is some feet below ground level but whose walls are pierced by a window sandbagged outside. A frightful bombing breaks out. Twice the window swings right in with the force of the blast. Twice I don my tin helmet and creep out to see the sky red with fire, to hear the sound of the planes overhead, to hear the ping of falling shrapnel, to see fires all along the city, and nearby houses and a church spire standing out as clearly as in an aquatint of moonlight.

Nancy Astor and I keep the company entertained below, but the business is not really funny. The windows in the front of the house are broken. After midnight, all clear sounds, and Admiral, Rootes & I go down to the city. A frightful scene. Street after street afire; furniture litters the footpaths; poor old people shocked & dazed are led along to shelter. The Guild Hall is a beacon of fire. Buildings blaze and throw out sparks like a bush fire. There are few fire appliances and firemen. Picture Melbourne blazing from Flinders to Lonsdale, from Swanston or Russell to Elizabeth Streets; with hundreds of back street houses burning as well. Every now & then a delayed action bomb explodes (two were so close as to make me duck) or a building collapses. Millions of pounds go west in an hour. I am in a grim sense glad to have seen it. I am all for peace when it comes, but it will be a tragedy for humanity if it comes before these beasts have had their own

---

137   Sir Henry Parkes, born near Coventry, emigrated to New South Wales in 1839 and was subsequently five times Premier of the colony. He has been popularly dubbed the 'Father of Australian Federation' for his role in bringing the representatives of the colonial governments together in conferences which framed a draft constitution for Australia.

138   Bridgwater.

139   Lady Astor, flamboyant American-born wife of Viscount Waldorf Astor, the first woman to take her seat in the House of Commons.

cities ravaged. The Hun must be made to learn through his hide; for sheer brutality this kind of thing is beyond the imagining of those who have not actually witnessed it. I thought it horrible, but Billy Rootes said "Nothing to Coventry!!"[140]

Saturday March 22nd

To Devonport Dockyards (D. is contiguous to Plymouth). See Gunnery schools, and repair depot, with several warships in dock under repair. Why do we persist in thinking that an Engineer Admiral or some such person can run a dockyards, which is a production business? These yards are a shambles—like a second hand machinery dealer's. I must speak to Alexander about it. It gave me (and Rootes) the uneasy idea that repairing warships may be taking twice as long as it should: and if this is so there are two disasters. The ship is longer in dock as a helpless target from the air; and she is missing too long from the vital battle of the Atlantic.

The smoke is rising from Plymouth as I go to see No 10 RAAF who are clearing up broken glass but O.K. (Don Cameron Flt St—present and well).

The church where Drake worshipped has gone. Old history's signs are destroyed. What will the new history say?

Cannot enter city of Plymouth today, public being excluded because of delayed action bombs. Hear that the Astor house, where we were to stay, was bombed!

Away to Stype[141] with Rootes where a quiet evening with W.S. Robinson[142] & Brendan Bracken, who admires and stoutly supports Cranborne.

Sunday March 23rd

To Portsmouth, much ruin as usual, in the central business portion of the city, including a magnificent but completely gutted Guild Hall. Visit dockyards with Admiral James ("Bubbles"),[143] see some Australian sailors,[144] and visit the

---

140   An Australian journalist described for the Australian public Menzies' party as they helped the victims of the Plymouth raid. 'We looked a queer lot to be the entourage of a Prime Minister. Some were unshaved, for reasons beyond our control. All were drooping from lack of sleep, with smoke-shot eyes and with hair and clothes filled with bomb dust. All had experienced every terror of night bombing.' *Sydney Morning Herald*, 24 March 1941.

141   'Stype Grange', near Hungerford in Berkshire, was the home of Billy Rootes.

142   William Sydney Robinson, influential Australian businessman and industrialist. He was a founding figure in the mining industry and creator of the Commonwealth Aircraft Corporation in 1936, an organisation designed to aid the development of Australian air defences.

143   Admiral Sir William James, Commander-in-Chief, Portsmouth.

144   Menzies told the sailors: 'Air raids are not going to defeat Britain. German soldiers are not going to land here successfully. The biggest job, therefore, rests with the Navy, which requires a big and concentrated effort, to which you men are expected to make a valuable contribution.' *Sydney Morning Herald*, 24 March 1941.

"Victory". She has a hole caused by a bomb. Between decks you must stoop, and on the deck where Nelson died you must bend almost double. They show you the place by the light of a horn lantern <u>by which the surgeon operated</u> in those days.

I see a delayed bomb being dug up, and try to look as if I felt safe.

Then to London & out to Chequers for dinner. Sir Andrew Duncan & Portal[145] present. The former is good & strong, but found Winston hard to pin on a business or economic matter; this is W's blind spot.

Monday March 24th

Routine. Lunch with Stirling. War Cabinet chiefly about Ireland, but also rendered gloomy by reports from Jugo-Slavia, Turkey and Spain. The Irish position grows intolerable. Winston summed up—"700 years of hatred, and six months of pure funk" There is some truth in this; they are terrified of attack, for which they have no preparation or defence, if neutrality is not strictly observed.

END OF DIARY 'B'; DIARY 'C' BEGINS

Tuesday March 25th

Conference on shipping and shipbuilding. They are interested & will send an expert ship builder to Australia. I make a berserk attack on Admiralty control of industrial operations such as ship repairs and have the undisguised support of Duncan & Cross.[146]

Speech at Hatchard's the Booksellers in Piccadilly on "The British Character".[147] Audience ranges from Maisky[148] to Margot Asquith,[149] who writes me enthusiastically afterwards "Your speech was perfect". So it must have been tolerable. Beverley Baxter spoke after me, and was richly diverting on the subject of "the absence of sportsmanship in cricket", which the Englishman has paradoxically (says B.B.) adopted as his standard of comparison. Longman's literary adviser wants to publish my speeches![150]

---

145   Air Chief Marshal, Sir Charles Portal, Chief of the Air Staff.

146   Menzies complained of the serious effects on the Australian economy of shipping shortages, urged that shipbuilding for merchant as well as naval purposes be developed in Australia and pointed to a need to improve ship repair services in Britain. War Cabinet, 25 March 1941, PRO CAB 99/4.

147   He referred to the British capacity for patience and fortitude. 'This magnificent courage [in adversity], born of tolerance, is what makes England home to me ... The essence of the present struggle is a battle against intolerance. All my liberties are inborn, and I do not want any Government to hand them out.' *Sydney Morning Herald*, 26 March 1941.

148   Ivan Maisky, Soviet Ambassador in London.

149   Emma Alice Margaret (Margot) Asquith, Countess of Oxford and Asquith.

150   Which they did do, under the title *To the People of Britain at War* (London, 1941).

Dine with J.P.L. Thomas, R.O. Law[151] (son of Bonar), Bowes-Lyon &c at Ritz and have good talk on post war reconstruction and the future of the Conservative Party.

Wednesday March 26th

Conference with Greenwood, Woolton, & Leith-Ross re export surpluses and the joint problem of storing what you cannot ship.

Then to Clothworkers Company, where I am given the Honorary Freedom & Livery (hereditary—so my sons can claim membership if they come here!) Respond briefly. Then lunch, where I speak to a pleased audience and to my surprise and delight am presented with a replica of a great Silver Tankard of 1684 which I had admired five minutes before, with a gold & enamel brooch for Pat.

Confer at War office regarding war effort, & find U.K. would like about 60 000 more troops for Army, corps, & bits & pieces. It is a stiff proposition, and I do not know.[152]

Then to N°.10, where Winston presides over a conference on "The Battle of the Atlantic". He is pale, unpleasant, and strained. All Ministers & service heads look and sound like 6th form boys in the presence of the headmaster. I wish I knew the secret! The battle of the Atlantic looks lousy, & privately I wish I had more _real_ faith in the navy.

Dine with the Duke & Duchess of Devonshire—Winant & Oliver Lyttelton. All in good form. Talk. The Oxford Group. Decision—hostile![153]

Thursday March 27th

More discussion at Supply Dept. Sir Andrew Duncan very encouraging about Australian production—quality first class, and balance of programme and magnitude of achievement astonishing! This means something from Duncan who is a hard-headed and I suspect humourless Scot, with lots of brains and courage.

Lunch with BBC (Powell,[154] Ogilvie[155] &c) and speak frankly on

---

151   Richard Kidston Law, Parliamentary Under-Secretary of State for Foreign Affairs.

152   At this meeting the Vice-Chief of the Imperial General Staff, General Sir Robert Haining, emphasised that the threat of invasion meant that few British troops could be spared to go abroad, and asked the Australians to provide the base units for AIF divisions in the field, such units having hitherto been made up of British troops. Shedden calculated that this would mean finding an extra 68 000 men almost at once. War Office Meeting, 26 March 1941, PRO CAB 99/44/1–13.

153   The Oxford Group, better known after 1938 as the Moral Rearmament movement, had many British adherents in this period. Its non-denominational revivalism, which advocated 'a changed life' through 'the guidance of God', was a matter for vigorous discussion in political and intellectual circles.

154   Sir George Allan Powell, Chairman of the BBC.

155   Frederick Wolff Ogilvie, Director-General of the BBC.

broadcasting matters. Chief themes, 1. Remember the clock is not the same everywhere. 2. Don't beat the British Government to a piece of news.

Press interview amusing, for Jugo-Slav revolution has just come, Prince "Palsy" has gone, young King Peter is on the throne, and we are all wishfully thinking that the tide has turned. Douglas says—à propos of the Jugo-Slav names—"It's hard to tell vitch vitch is vitch" and also—"Ah! Robbing Paul to pay Peter!"[156]

War Cabinet more cheerful as a result. Afterwards movie pictures of AI,[157] glider torpedoes &c &c.

Friday March 28th

Conference at Dept. Information. Duff Cooper presides with dullness and disinterest. A queer fellow, with a dead face and I should think great gifts of indolence. Censorship same as ours, except that in all matters of difference the <u>Service</u> prevails, subject to Cabinet decision. Interesting and vigorous discussion re BBC "scooping" Government announcements, & we are assured that new liaison arrangements will obviate such trouble in future.

Lunch with Geoffrey Dawson,[158] Ogilvie, & Herbert Asquith.[159] The latter rather like his father in a faded and "gangling" way. Subject Ireland. This country must not just drift into an Irish war.

Conference at Admiralty—Alexander still impresses me as knowledgeable and practical. Got some results.

Saturday March 29th

After a good morning's work on documents, have a look at East End and Docks area. Docks have suffered and seem strangely silent but several ships are berthed, and business, modified, goes on. Surrounding areas almost evacuated. Facades of terraces stand, but thousands of houses gutted or vacant. Then to Chequers where I find Winant, the American Ambassador, and Harriman, dark,

---

156   Diplomatic attempts to persuade Prince Paul, Prince Regent of Jugoslavia since 1934, to resist Axis pressure, had failed. In March 1941 the fearful Paul, dubbed 'Prince Palsy' by Churchill, had reluctantly made a pact with the Axis. This, aided by British diplomatic stirring, inspired anti-German forces in Belgrade to stage a military coup, and on 26 March the young King Peter II was declared ruler. The Germans responded in April by bombing Belgrade and occupying the country. Channon, a great supporter of Prince Paul, later blamed Menzies for the witticism: 'His Yugoslavian mot about "robbing Paul to pay Peter" has gone around London; it always irritates me.' *Chips*, p. 298.

157   Airborne Intercept—a type of radar used in fighters to detect enemy bombers.

158   Geoffrey Dawson, editor of *The Times*.

159   Herbert ('Beb') Asquith, the second son of Herbert Henry Asquith, British Prime Minister from 1908 to 1916.

good looking and much in favour of U.S.A. making such a declaration as will keep the peace in the Far East.[160]

Winston in good form—naval victory in Mediterranean,[161] added to Jugoslavia and Keren. He dictates a cable to Fadden in my presence. Paces up and down in a jerky way while his typist (80 hours a week and 80 words a minute) types direct from dictation. Before pronouncing the phrase aloud, Winston whispers it to himself, quite audibly, to "try the effect!" For the rest, we mostly listen, since somebody must![162]

Sunday March 30th

Good talk to Harriman (dark, tall, good-looking, Anglophile but with no illusions, and with a soft voice) and Winant, in W's bedroom, the Ambassador sitting up in bed. Both men have something to say about the bureaucrats here, and admire men like Churchill and Beaverbrook who can cut through the red tape. The old problem—files or performance; we know something of it in Australia.

At lunch Duke & Duchess of Kent. She in green ostrich feather hat and a brown suit. She has a markedly foreign accent, is devastatingly pretty, except that her eyes have nothing like the freshness and attractiveness of the Queen's, but I thought did not carry herself remarkably well. Keen on going to Australia, but I think would lack "the common touch".

Much photography in the grounds.[163] Great news of naval victory in Mediterranean at which Winston sends off cables to Roosevelt. Also a pretty direct letter (per Shigamitsu, to Matsuoka).[164] What a genius the man

---

160   W. Averell Harriman had come to England as President Roosevelt's special envoy to organise the supply of equipment.

161   The sinking off Cape Matapan of three Italian cruisers and two destroyers. Churchill called it, 'the tearing up of the paper fleet of Italy'. *Fringes*, pp. 439–40.

162   Churchill's message to Fadden registered unreal euphoria: the Greek campaign, it could now be seen, was truly justified. 'When a month ago we decided upon LUSTRE it looked a rather bleak military adventure dictated by noblesse oblige. Thursday's events in Belgrade show far-reaching effects of this and other measures we have taken on whole Balkan situation. German plans have been upset and we may cherish renewed hopes of forming a Balkan front with Turkey comprising about 70 Allied divisions from the four powers concerned ... everything that has happened since Lustre decision taken justifies it ... Result unknowable but prize has increased and risks have somewhat lessened. Am in closest touch with Menzies. Wish I could talk it over with you.' Churchill to Fadden, 31 March 1941, PRO CAB 65/18/54.

163   Colville also describes the lunch party: 'Afterwards the Duke inspected the Guard while I struggled with his chauffeur-less car and the Duchess. Mr Menzies photographed the proceedings assiduously ... Sarah came to tea and there was more photography by Mr Menzies.' *Fringes*, p. 439.

164   Mamoru Shigemitsu, Japanese Ambassador to the United Kingdom since 1938. Yosuke Matsuoka, the Japanese Foreign Minister.

has. He has maintained by cable and letter the most easy and informal correspondence with Roosevelt; always treating him as a friend and ally, and also U.S.A.—

"Don't you think <u>we</u> could do so and so". Result, F.D.R. has passed into the position of an ally without perhaps realising how some of the steps have come about. Letter to Matsuoka is direct series of questions about how Japan would fare in a war—refreshing stuff after the evasions of the Foreign Office.

Harriman tells me he regards a double shuttle (us supply USA West Coast and they supplying Great Britain) as reasonable; and thinks I can get it if I press in Washington.

Monday March 31st

Longman's representative has offered to publish my speeches. I am to look see to find out if I have enough which are up to the mark.

Saw Betty Kendrick (Bellair)[165] who is bright and cheerful & courageous—a grand advertisement for Australia. Her husband was at Dunkirk.

War Cabinet. Sinkings are still very grave. But great compensation in the news of the naval victory in the Mediterranean.

Winston's attitude to war is much more realistic than mine. I constantly find myself looking at "minor losses" and saying "There are some darkened homes". But he is wise. War is terrible and it cannot be won except by lost lives. That being so, don't think of them.

He is sending a letter to Matsuoka at Lisbon—a series of interrogations about Japan's prospects of winning a war against us (<u>and</u> America). Good direct stuff, shocking to the Foreign Office but pleasing to me.[166]

Tuesday April 1st

Walk down a wet and almost deserted Bond Street and do a little shopping. Interview Chancellor of the Exchequer regarding optional redemption loans. Kingsley Wood is small, rotund, gold-chained, and intelligent, but he is at present hag-ridden by his impending Budget, and, while undoubtedly capable, is too lacking in personality or presence to be a great Minister.

---

165 Betty Kenrick (Bellair).

166 As Colville reports this message: 'He begins by asking: "Will Germany, without the command of the sea or the command of the British daylight air, be able to invade and conquer Great Britain in the spring, summer or autumn of 1941? Will Germany try to do so? Would it not be in the interests of Japan to wait until these questions have answered themselves?" He asks seven other equally pertinent questions and concludes: "From the answers to these questions may spring the avoidance by Japan of a serious catastrophe, and a marked improvement in the relations between Japan and the two great sea powers of the West." ' *Fringes*, p. 440.

Lunch in city with Athol Lewis[167]—as amusing as ever. Venue—the Pickwick Room at the George and Vulture, where I meet half a dozen discount and re-insurance brokers, have a grilled chop (mirabile dictu) and am presented with an ancient pewter pot.

Feeling very homesick and depressed. London's savour has gone. A city living in the darkness is queer, and life becomes formless.

Wednesday April 2nd

To London Fire Brigade with Herbert Morrison; splendid display of fire-fighting methods &c, and a parade of Civil Defence Services, addressed, in spite of the echo from the loud-speakers opposite, by Morrison & myself.

Lunch with Storey, Fedden (chief engine designer Bristol, and man of rare intelligence) and Rowbotham (engine production Bristol). These men are interested in Australia.

Taken at night by Mrs Randolph Churchill to my solitary party—at Claridges, where I as usual fail to dance but have good talk with various, from Diana Cooper to Mrs Montague (of Asquith's letters).[168]

Tomorrow to Ireland![169]

Thursday April 3rd

Cold journey by DH "Flamingo" from Hendon to Belfast, over Isle of Man and across a wind-tossed and bitter Irish Sea.

Belfast cold and blowy. Received by Andrews P.M.,[170] smallish but intelligent and I should think of a more flexible mind than Craigavon.[171]

---

167   Athol Lewis, a contemporary of Menzies' at Wesley College, was an older brother of Phyllis Lewis to whom Menzies was briefly engaged while he and she were both prominently involved in student activities at Melbourne University.

168   Colville noted: 'Glamorous pay-party at Claridges ... There has been nothing like it since the war ... It was wonderful to see a display of real evening dresses again and to meet people I had not seen since 1939. All London was there and the gaiety was great.' *Fringes*, p. 441. Mrs Montagu was born Venetia Stanley, sister of Sir Arthur Stanley, Governor of Victoria 1914–20. When Asquith was Prime Minister he had conducted an indiscreet affair with her and he later published some of their very extensive correspondence in his *Memories and Reflections, 1852–1927* (Alexander Mackintosh (ed), 1928). In 1915 Venetia married the wealthy Edwin Montagu, Asquith's former private secretary and devoted admirer.

169   For a discussion of the visit that follows and its consequences for Menzies, see Appendix II 'The Trip to Ireland'.

170   John Miller Andrews, Prime Minister of Northern Ireland.

171   Lord Craigavon (James Craig). Under the Government of Ireland Act he became the first Prime Minister of Northern Ireland in 1921 and remained Prime Minister until his death in 1940.

Menzies leaves a warship after a tour of inspection at Plymouth. (Menzies Papers)

Menzies shares a joke with a sergeant of the Royal Australian Air Force at a southern coastal command. (Menzies Papers)

A grim-faced group of Air Force officers waits while Menzies films bomb damage. (AWM 6687)

Accompanied by Herbert Morrison, Minister for Home Security, Menzies inspects Air Raid Precaution equipment at a parade of London's Civil Defence. (Menzies Papers)

Menzies with the Prime Minister of Eire, Eamon de Valera, in Dublin. (Menzies Film)

King George VI, the Queen and the young Princess Elizabeth. (Menzies Film)

Menzies leaves Buckingham Palace after an audience with the King. (Menzies Papers)

Menzies with Lloyd George. (Menzies Film)

Winston Churchill with Menzies in the grounds of Chequers. (Menzies Film)

At a reception in his honour at the Overseas Club, St James, Menzies chats with Australian soldiers and sailors. (Menzies Papers)

Bomb damage in a Bristol street. (Menzies Film)

Inspect Harland & Woolf[172] shipyards, where at any given moment they have about 100 ships under construction, repair, or refit. About 30 000 employees. Also Short & Harland where they are making Short Stirling Bombers. Lunch at Ulster Reform Club, & speak to a record attendance. They acclaim my speech in extravagant terms. Then to a really splendid Parliament House at Stormont, where we have tea and a reception. Andrews has instituted 4 Salaried Parlty Secretaries, with defined duties & with success. The P.M.'s house is an old castle, partly occupied by offices, while the Speaker has a fine red-brick Georgian House in the grounds. Few R.C. members sit, because there is a law requiring the oath of allegiance.

Receive Hon LL.D. of Queen's University, Belfast & carry away certificate and loot as souvenirs.

Then to Government House (Duke & Duchess of Abercorn[173]—very good!) for the night. Up here they say "we are of a different race from the South"—but query? There is little logic. I will put my political observations into a memorandum for Churchill.

Recruiting is bad—fear that Southerners may come in and take their job?

Friday April 4th

Down to Dublin by train, per the Boyne and Drogheda! Countryside quite lovely, the white washed cottages making quite a picture in the greenery. In Dublin life goes on and there is no blackout—it seems queer!

Long conference, followed by lunch, with Devalera. Long, long grey black frieze overcoat, broad brimmed black hat. An educated man. Personal charm. Allusions to history, but not all ancient. He and all his ministers have "done time" as rebels, and family blood has been spilt in the streets. We must remember this—"You have not died on the Barricades"!

In afternoon, out with Sean T. O'Kelly[174]—grey headed and swarthy with Father Costello, a worldly priest, to Wicklow mountains & lovely ruins & lakes of Glendalough. Dine at Hunter's Hotel where I meet a Digger poet, & then to various houses—"Paddy" Murphy—Potheen.

Saturday April 5th

Drive around Dublin with Beeton of Irish External Affairs. A bigot. O'Connell[175] (late Sackville) Street. The Nelson Column—"He was not an

---

172   Harland & Wolff.

173   Duke of Abercorn, Governor of Northern Ireland since 1922.

174   Sean Thomas O'Kelly, Minister of Finance and Minister of Education, Eire, was one of the founders of Sinn Fein.

175   O'Connell Street, renamed after Daniel O'Connell, 'The Liberator', who had secured Catholic emancipation for Ireland in 1829.

Irishman", Phoenix Park. The Wellington statue. "To be born in a stable does not prove you are a horse".[176]

Lunch with Cabinet, and Dev sees me off at aerodrome. Rough journey in a "Rapide" to Liverpool and to Heston. Pilot thinks we are pursued in Irish Channel. We grope our way into Heston through fog and balloons.

Dine at Euston Fire Brigade, and then to a Refuge & Shelter at Bermondsey, where I address a couple of hundred inmates. Success.

Sunday April 6th

To Cherkley, Beaverbrook's house. He is clear headed and forceful. Others present Bruce Lochart,[177] Michael Foott,[178] Patricia Ward & Lord Castlerosse.[179] A quaint bag. Note B's love of scandal and direct language.

Monday April 7th

Lunch with Gavin Simonds[180] (greetings to Pat) & Lord Herbert Scott (Rolls Royce). At War Cabinet. Things have gone wrong in Libya.[181] Wavell's estimate of possible attack from Tripoli grossly falsified, and we are in danger of inadequate retreat & grave loss. Wish my people in Australia would hang to central idea of helping Greece, and would not assume that I am not raising obvious points about equipment &c.

Dine with Winant & Harriman. W. is quite amusing when you get to know him. T. Roosevelt's son said of him "The old man always wants to be in the picture. He wants to be the bride at a wedding, or the corpse at a funeral!"

---

176   In his biographical memoir, *Afternoon Light*, Menzies explains these somewhat enigmatic notes of his meeting with Beeton ('Mr X'). Referring to the Nelson Monument in O'Connell Street, Mr X said, ' "and I'll not need to tell you that many of us think that it should have been removed." ' Menzies retorted: ' "And what did Nelson ever do to you, except save you from Napoleon, in common with the rest of us?" His reply was splendid, complete and crushing. "Sir, he was not an Irishman!" … Over-eager to recover some of my lost ground, I said "Ah! There is Wellington! You can't say he wasn't an Irishman, … he was born on the premises!" That proved to be my swan-song. For Mr X had the last word. "And wasn't it Wellington himself who said that to be born in a stable didn't argue that you were a horse?" ' p. 43.

177   R.H. Bruce Lockhart, writer and diplomat, had previously worked for Beaverbrook on the *Evening Standard*. Now Deputy Secretary of State in the Foreign Office, he directed the Political Warfare Executive which coordinated propaganda in enemy and enemy-occupied countries.

178   Michael Foot, radical politician and journalist, was then a young protégé of Beaverbrook.

179   Lord Castlerosse wrote a famous gossip column between 1926 and 1939 in the *Sunday Express* entitled 'Londoner's Log'.

180   Sir Gavin Simonds, Judge of Chancery Division, High Court of Justice, and Chairman of the National Arbitration Tribunal.

181   See Appendix I 'The Greek Campaign'.

It is a mistake to think Americans love the English; they don't, even while they admire them. But they like Australians.

Tuesday April 8th

See Noel Heath. O.K. Lunch with Walter Elliott,[182] who sends greetings to the Wakehursts.[183] Elliott is Relation officer to War Office. "Oh what a fall was there, my countryman".

Audience with King, who is a little subdued. Moved when I said farewell and good fortune, "from 7 million Australians".

Conference at F.O., where my argument about "chalk-line" for Japan has taken root, and good may result.

Prepare memo. on Irish position. Dine with Vincent Masseys,[184] who enquire after Pat.

War Cabinet at night. Balkans bad. O'Connor & Neame missing in Libya. The clouds are dark and there is a lurid patch in the sky—I hope not sunset. As I write, guns in Hyde Park are firing. Last night Belfast had its first raid, and the aero works I inspected on Thursday destroyed!

The generals of the War Office are still behind the times. "We have so many divisions"—as if divisions counted. Armour and speed count, and when we catch up to that idea, we will catch up to the Germans.

Only tonight I was horrified to hear Churchill saying, à propos of Tobruk to which we are retreating and where we hope to make a stand, "If stout hearted men with rifles cannot hold these people until the guns come up, I must revise my ideas of war". Well, he should revise them quickly!

Wednesday April 9th

To House of Commons, to hear Winston explain Libya, Greece and the Battle of the Atlantic. Not a good speech. He was earth-bound and hesitating, and failed to electrify the House. But even then managed a good phrase "and then, the sword of retribution in our hands, we shall be after him!" He announces fall of Salonika & Massawa, both of which he had saved up for a day!! Speak at Grosvenor House to American Outposts Society—on "The People's War". I think the theme was good.

See Beaverbrook and have good talk regarding aircraft production. B. is active concise and knowledgeable, hates red tape, and grows on me. He is, like me,

---

182   Walter Elliot, Conservative MP and former minister in the Chamberlain Government, now Director of Public Relations at the War Office. He had at one time been seen as a future prime minister.

183   Lord Wakehurst was Governor of New South Wales.

184   Vincent Massey, Canadian High Commissioner in London since 1935.

concerned about the failure to understand mechanisation. Men should be taken out of the infantry and put into the production of tanks—heavy and fast ones at that! These generals have let us down—the Germans are too clever for them.

Send in my memorandum on the Irish position as I see it.

Beginning already to clear up outstanding matters for the return home.

Thursday April 10th

Good talk Sinclair & Beaverbrook re Aircraft for Australia. I think they are treating us fairly, but Shedden imagines that our risks in Australia are as great as those here. I do not agree.[185]

War Cabinet re Ireland. Winston describes my paper as "very readable"—a most damning comment. Beaverbrook, Sinclair & Greenwood rather approve, but Winston & Kingsley Wood exhibit the blank wall of conservatism. There is triangular prejudice on this matter. Winston is not a receptive or reasoning animal. But they will come to it!

Do a broadcast (War Loan, Australia) at a battered BBC House. I like Ogilvie—then to Transport House to T.U.C. Gibson[186] and Citrine.[187] We exchange speeches. In mine I dwell on "No status quo, but a world in which, if there is power, as there will be, it is shared and not the prerogative of a few".

Confer with Greenwood, Woolton and Wood on surpluses. Greenwood really grateful for Australia's attitude & Woolton helpful. Dine with Bruce & Ethel at Palace Gardens, SMB[188] in a siren suit!!

Friday April 11th (Good Friday)

War Cabinet to hear Eden & Dill. Eden gave a coherent and indeed lucid account of his negotiations in the Middle East, but I cannot see him as of sufficient tonnage to be P.M. Dill is I think good; does not dodge the issue. Libya represents a gross underestimate of German capacity. Tobruk is a poor place to defend, with an extended perimeter but Dill thinks the supply of anti-tank guns and field artillery quite good. He assures me that as

---

185   Menzies asked for a British undertaking that fifty-four Beaufighters should be made
       available for Australian defence but Sinclair wanted aircraft to be progressively released
       to Australia after December 1941. Menzies accepted, 'on the understanding that if war
       spread to the Far East, the Australian Government might have to send out an urgent call
       for aircraft'. War Cabinet, Meeting at Ministry for Aircraft Production, 10 April 1941,
       PRO CAB 99/4.

186   George Gibson, Chairman of the Trades Union Congress.

187   Sir Walter McLennan Citrine, General Secretary of the Trades Union Congress.

188   Stanley Melbourne Bruce.

many armoured divisions as humanly possible are being formed, and that Germany has only 15 out of 200![189]

Cross examine the First Sea Lord a good deal about naval power and our failure to cut off Tripoli. Explanation—the dive bomber, based on Sicily and Tripoli renders the water unsafe except to submarines, our fighters based on Malta have too short a range to contact the bombers.

More bombing of aircraft factories in England. The Hun is becoming too accurate, and picking our factories off too regularly.

After lunch, to Oxford, Burford, Withington (W.S. Morrison) and then to Lydney, where we stay overnight with Lord Bledisloe[190] and meet Lord & Lady Raglan.

<u>Saturday April 12th</u> Cross the strong brown tide of the Severn by ferry and to Bristol, still smoking from a <u>blitz</u> last night. Winston, as Chancellor, confers LL.D degrees on Winant & myself. A fine ceremony. The great hall has been destroyed some time ago, and we meet in a room under the great tower. Winston's speech unprepared, and the best I have heard him make. Winant & I also spoke.[191]

Then handed over to Lord Mayor Underdown Mobile Canteen on behalf of head office of AMP[192] (of which Bledisloe is a London director). Lord Mayor then gives me a luncheon, at which I speak on the troubles ahead and the need to "follow our leader".

Bristol a sad sight—churches blazing and streets of houses in ruins but St Mary Radcliffe,[193] the "fairest church in Christendom" of Elizabeth, stands untouched among the ruins. So I must say, seemed also the spirit of the university, where many a gown was worn over working uniform, and many learned participants had been up fire-fighting all night.

---

189   Menzies complained in Cabinet that Wavell had gravely underestimated the capacity of German armoured divisions and declared that the perimeter of Tobruk was too large and scattered to be strongly held by the relatively small garrison now there. War Cabinet, 11 April 1941, PRO CAB 65/18/77. Channon reported (11 April): 'Rab accompanied Anthony Eden to the Cabinet to hear his apologies: certainly he has brought back nothing but disaster. The military were much criticised, particularly by Menzies, it seems, who was present.' *Chips*, p. 299.

190   Lord Bledisloe (Charles Bathurst) was a former Governor-General of New Zealand, 1930–35. 'Lydney Park', his family estate, was in Gloucestershire. According to Colville, George V called him 'Lord Bloody-Slow'. *Fringes*, p. 76.

191   Colville notes in his diary Churchill's 'excellent impromptu speech'. In a footnote he recounts: 'Menzies, who spoke poorly on this occasion, told me afterwards that he never spoke with notes. He always found it was politically more impressive, and seldom risky, to speak impromptu. In this discovery he was luckier than most politicians.' *Fringes*, p. 444.

192   Australian Mutual Provident Society.

193   St Mary Redcliffe.

Back per Withington and Fairford to Oxford, where we dine at the Mitre. I am now recognised wherever I go, and autograph books are produced. And so to London.

<u>Sunday April 13th</u>   A little photography about the city, and then to "Coppins" to the Duke & Duchess of Kent (+ Nancy Astor + Philip Sassoon's sister + Jugo-Slav Minister). She (the Duchess) is sorely tried by the events in the Balkans. (She is Greek and her sister is the wife of the feeble Prince Paul of JugoSlavia). The two children are most good-looking and full of beans.

Then to Cliveden, where I have a good talk with Astor and J.L. Garvin[194] (imperiously summonsed from Beaconsfield for the conference) on Mechanisation & Ireland. On the latter, Garvin declared my "memorandum" as "the most penetrating account of the Irish position he had ever read".

Then to Chequers, where Harriman also present, but we are all depressed by the news of what I call the "botch" in Libya.[195]

<u>Monday April 14th</u>

The position in Libya becomes worse, and Egypt is threatened. In Balkans, the Jugo-Slavs are going to collapse, and as the Greeks have not withdrawn their Albanian divisions, the Aliakhmon line will probably be turned and our Greek position rendered untenable.

At War Cabinet, W.C. speaks at length as the Master-Strategist—"Tobruk <u>must</u> be held as a bridge-head or rally post, from which to hit the enemy". "With what?" says I, and so the discussion goes on. Wavell and the Admiralty have failed us. The Cabinet is deplorable—dumb men most of whom disagree with Winston but none of whom dare to say so. This state of affairs is most dangerous. The Chiefs of Staff are without exception Yes Men, and a politician runs the services. Winston is a dictator; he cannot be overruled, and his colleagues fear him. The people have set him up as something little less than God, and his power is therefore terrific.

Today I decide to remain for a couple of weeks, for grave decisions will have to be taken about M.E., chiefly Australian forces, and I am not content to have them solved by "unilateral rhetoric".

---

194   Lord Astor had been a Conservative MP from 1910 until 1919. On succeeding to his father's title he was forced to resign his seat of Plymouth, which was won by his wife Lady Astor, but he continued to take a close interest in politics. His home, 'Cliveden', located mid-way between Oxford and London, was a meeting place during the late 1930s for Neville Chamberlain and his supporters. As proprietor of the *Observer* Astor worked closely with J.L. Garvin, its politically influential editor since 1908.

195   A reference to Wavell's miscalculation of the number of troops needed to hold the Benghazi front. See Appendix I 'The Greek Campaign'.

<u>Tuesday April 15th</u>

Conference re Pan Pacific airways and Australia. Routine work.

At night, entertain about 50 men to dinner. Practically all Cabinet except PM, the Chiefs of Staff, H. Comd^r, A-Generals &c. A cheery party, at which I make a wicked speech about the Chiefs of Staff; thank God the speech is, by those present, understood to be funny.[196]

Tobruk is holding out and Sollum is recaptured pro tem, but the cutting of supplies to Tripoli is the only hope. The navy must take great risks to do this.

<u>Wednesday April 16th</u> "Times" welcomes my remaining in London for a time. I have mixed feelings—desperately homesick—go out and buy Heather a pearl necklace—it will always be good, and a fine souvenir.

Call at U.S. Embassy, and see Mrs Winant—vivacious, with a nervous "tic" in the face. When J.G.W. (who likes me!) arrived he said "Ah! each of you is in good company!"

Tonight the enemy is passing overhead. You can hear him. The search lights are operating—and the crack of the guns in the park opposite is deafening. To look out of window you switch out the lights and peep through the curtain. An eerie experience, the sky occasionally flashing like lightning with the explosion of the A.A. shells. London is so vast that the German bombers pass over it on their way to any of the Midland or Northern cities. But how many A.A. shells are fired per hit God only knows. While the uproar goes on the buses and taxis still rumble along Park Lane!

<u>Later.</u> I was wrong. They were not passing. 460 of them were attacking London, and a dozen large bombs fell within 100 yards of the Dorchester. It was a terrible experience. Invited up to the second floor for a drink with two elderly ladies (one of them John Lowther's mother), we had scarcely sat down when a great explosion and blast shattered the windows of the room, blew the curtains in, split the door, and filled the room with acrid fumes. Twice the whole building seemed to bounce with the force of the concussion. Twice I visited the ground floor, and found it full of white-faced people. Tritton went out to escort a guest home, got into the blitz, had his taxi driver wounded and the wind-screen broken, and took the wheel himself!

The sky beyond the Palace was red with fire and smoke, the sky was flashing like lightning. It is a horrible sound to hear the whistle of a descending stick of bombs, any one of them capable of destroying a couple of five-storey houses, and to wonder for a split second if it is going to land on your windows!

---

196 Channon also attended: 'I dined with Bob Menzies, and went with Jay Llewellin and Harold, not expecting so brilliant a gathering, as we found fifty men, all the Government, Simon and Portal, etc.' *Chips*, p. 300.

Just before dawn, at about 5 a.m., Tritton, Landau and I went for a walk to see the damage. There were buildings down and great craters within 100 yards of the hotel on the side away from the park. In Brook Street buildings were blazing. A great plume of red smoke rose from Selfridge's. Gas mains blazed in Piccadilly. The houses fronting the Green Park were red and roaring. There were craters and fallen masonry in the streets, and the fear of an unexploded bomb lurking around every corner. Wherever we walked, we crunched over acres of broken glass. This is the "new order". How can it go on for years?

<u>Thursday April 17</u>th   It takes a long time to reach Downing Street. All round Victoria there is damage and confusion. The Admiralty has a great chunk cut out of it. Charing Cross Station is ablaze, and the Halifax Building in the Strand also. Shell-Mex building has a great unexploded bomb, and is evacuated. Two bombs fell on either side of the street from Australia House. In Middle London, every street shows the marks. There are at least 1000 dead and 2000 seriously injured.[197] Opposite the Dorchester I see in the Park, not 100 yards away, the craters of the stick of bombs which I <u>felt</u> last night.

5 bombers were destroyed out of 460. We must do better than this if we are to defeat him.

Lord & Lady Stamp[198] were killed. I see many people who are drawn, black under the eyes, and shaken. After maintaining cheerfulness last night, I feel very "off" myself.

War news mixed. The position at Tobruk seems better. The navy has disposed of an entire Tripoli convoy of 5 ships and 3 destroyers. The Jugs have gone, and preparations are in hand for an evacuation of Greece!

The heroes of these frightful attacks are the police, the firemen (working nearest the glare, which is the target), and the taxi drivers!

On all averages, we shall have another tonight!

<u>Friday April 18</u>th

Well, we didn't. The evening was quiet. But London is a mess. All around Jermyn Street—Dunhills down to Christies, is ruined. The embankment is closed, and traffic is jammed into unaccustomed routes. There is a natural question—why bomb Berlin and have to claim that "the roof of the Library was damaged" or "the Opera House was destroyed" when the Hun can so obviously

---

197   'In the raids on London on 16th and 17th April, over 2,300 people were killed and more than 3,000 seriously injured.' Footnote in Nigel Nicolson (ed), *Harold Nicolson: Diaries and Letters 1939–1945* (London, 1967), p. 163.

198   Lord Stamp, economist and statistician, was the Government Adviser on Economic Co-ordination.

give London much more? Why not concentrate on military objectives until our bomb power is greater? Could London's nerves stand three consecutive nights of such wide-spread and obviously terroristic bombing as that of Wednesday night? How I admire the courage of the women, who do men's work under fire and are cheerful about it!

Greece goes badly, but Tobruk, thanks to Australia, well. I must insist upon Australians getting proper commands, for I have more confidence in them than I have in Wavell & Co., whose gross miscalculations have brought us to this pass.

Saturday April 19th

Long and frank talk with Dill, in which I take up question of Australian commands. (a) Blamey should be given a command, e.g. Western Desert, instead of some unknown Major General with a hyphen in his name. (b) Wavell's staff shd contain a senior Australian officer.

Dill, who is agreeable, but I think lacks iron in the system, agrees, and I am hopeful. It would be some offset to the inevitable yelling of the yellow-bellies in Australia—thank God a minority, but noisy, and with access to the press.

Lunch with Noel Coward,[199] and then up to Welbeck Abbey, near Newark—Duke of Portland—to see the Sydney Smiths, who are in grand form, though Clare's complaints about Sydney's non-promotion are becoming a fixation, and do him no good.

Sunday April 20th

Welbeck a lovely place—beautiful wrought iron and gardens. Curious tunnels and an underground ball-room built by an ancestor with more money than sense. Duchess a faded beauty but a Sargent portrait shows how lovely she was. Tells me how a burst water pipe flooded the ball-room and she wanted to jump in. "Rather chic to bathe in your ball-room!" House full of a magpie accumulation. An old-fashioned pair, and I like them. Out in the sunken garden there is a "temple" or shelter with a moving inscription saying that the Duke & Duchess sat there together on August 4th 1914 sorely anxious in spirit, and that they sat together once more on Nov 11th 1918 and gave thanks for the deliverance of England and the safety of their sons and brothers.

Now they pay 19/6 in the £ tax, are plainly living on capital, and their sons will see the passing of the old gracious and spacious days. Sic transit. There will

---

199   Noel Coward, playwright, actor and song-writer. He and Menzies had met in 1940 when
       Coward toured Australia. He published a slim volume of his broadcasts entitled
       Australia Visited, 1940 (London, 1941) which he dedicated 'to R.G. Menzies gratefully
       and with admiration from Noel Coward'.

be much of it. Perhaps, if I reach a ripe age, I will be a curio because I once lived a few week-ends in great country houses of England.

Drive through London to Fisher's Gate where Buck de la Warr & Diana are very friendly and ask warmly after Pat. Also present Lord Knollys[200] (NOLES) and Young Kitty and Harry Sackville—the latter 18 pale tall & elegant and a stern unbending Tory!

Monday April 21st   War Cabinet. Greece Evacuation talk. Dill has heard from Wavell, who speaks highly of Blamey, who has conducted the retreat to Thermopylae. Is willing to make him Deputy Commander in Chief Middle East!

Lunch Winston, Eden, Attlee & self under Cabinet Room at No. 10. Very amusing. I tell Winston he needs Chiefs of Staff who will tell him he is talking nonsense. W. explodes, but it draws him, and he reveals his real opinion of the Chiefs of Staff in terms I could not have equalled! He knows they are Yes-men, and does not love them for it.

Dine with Rootes Bros & Storey & W.S. Robinson re 'plane manufacture in Australia, W.S. is out to protect the C.A.C.[201] interests.

Tuesday April 22nd

Bombardment of Tripoli not, I think, a great success, but some damage done. We must turn this tap off if we are to save Egypt. Lunch with Gubby Allen and David Bowes-Lyon—the Queen's brother, and a clear-headed younger Tory PPS.[202]

Make a press statement for Australia, to steady the malcontents. Winston speaks to me on phone, and is disturbed at the way in which reported statements in Australia are adversely affecting Australia's reputation. Evatt's criticisms have been published here, and have done harm.[203] Prepare a broadcast for Australia to overtake this kind of thing.

Dine at Putney with Athol Lewis & Elsie. Youngsters are apparently pretty intelligent but they are of necessity skilled listeners. Drive home during an alarm, with gun flashes like lightning all about. Wear a tin hat in the car.

---

200   Lord Knollys ('Edgey'), businessman and Deputy Commissioner for Civil Defence, South-eastern Region.

201   Commonwealth Aircraft Corporation.

202   Parliamentary Private Secretary.

203   Dr H.V. Evatt, Labor member of the Advisory War Council, had publicly complained that the War Council had not been consulted on the transfer of the AIF to Greece, and had suggested that the decision should never have been made: 'it was not right to give a small force a task which was impossible because of its support equipment being unequal to that of the enemy.' The Times, 22 April 1941.

Wednesday April 23rd

Broadcast to Australia, in an endeavour to "stop the rot".[204] Widely reported in press here, and will do good here, if not in Australia. How can an Australian P.M. do any good here if his rear is unprotected and unsafe. Efforts must be renewed for a National Government.

Lunch with Colonel Menzies[205]—a garrulous but nice old man.

Greek position goes from bad to worse.

Dine with McGeaghs—he looks younger than ever.

Thursday April 24th

War Cabinet, at which I urge and emphasise air assistance to the full to cover retreat. I am afraid of a disaster, and understand less than ever why Dill and Wavell advised that the Greek adventure had _military_ merits. Of the moral merits I have no doubt. Better Dunkirk than Poland or Czechoslovakia.

Lunch Admiral Royle,[206] our new First Naval Member. He is not clever, and does not appear to grapple with large issues, but he is honest and determined and should do well.

See Kim and Shiela Mackay. He was in Australia only a fortnight ago and saw Pat about a month ago. Reports she is working too hard, and is worried about things. Still, he thinks my position is stronger than ever.

J.L. Price's death reported. Will Labour fight the seat, or will it prefer stability of government? The answer will depend upon its understanding of the present crisis.[207]

Dine interestingly with Philip Swinton, who speaks warmly of Pat. She has many warm admirers here.

---

204   'The momentous question of whether we should go to Greece,' Menzies explained, 'was the subject of extensive communications between the Governments of Australia, Great Britain, and New Zealand ... and the best advice was obtained from the generals who were on the spot.' He acknowledged that it was 'a hazardous undertaking' but he believed that 'to desert the Greeks ... would have been one of the infamies of history'. _Argus_, 24 April 1941.

205   Colonel Menzies was not a relation.

206   Vice-Admiral Sir Guy C.C. Royle, RN, First Naval Member of the Commonwealth Naval Board, from 21 April 1941.

207   With both major parties holding an equal number of seats and the balance of power resting with the two Independents, the vacation of J.L. Price's Boothby seat was critical for the Australian Government and for Menzies. He reveals here what the meaning of his subsequent protest about a by-election contest was: Price was a United Australia Party member (ex-Labor who had changed to the UAP as a result of the Depression crisis), and Menzies believed that national unity required Labor to accept the status quo and not contest the seat. In the upshot, it did; only to be defeated by the election of the UAP candidate, Archibald Grenfell Price. But in the meantime, Menzies had agonised about the contest, to his great personal and political disadvantage, as a failure to match the spirit of wartime unity evident, he maintained, in Britain.

Friday April 25th

Anzac Day. Lay a wreath on Cenotaph, and walk up Whitehall with Birdwood,[208] who looks quite young and brisk. Service at St. Martin's in the Fields, where I read the first lesson. St Clement's Danes not useable because of bombing.

Anzac Lunch at Overseas Club (half of which is bombed out!) with Milne[209] in the chair. A moving speech by the Greek Minister. A speech by me.[210]

Clearing up outstanding matters before leaving for home next week.

At dusk, visit Air Raid Shelters in the <u>Tubes</u> at King's Cross and Old Street. Indescribably pathetic. Malodorous, or rather stuffy. Bunks of wire arranged in tiers of 2 or 3 along the platforms and in the recesses. Canteen arranged. Little children staggering in beneath bundles of bed-clothes. Old women & men, going down to their nightly burial, for this happens every night, and not just when the alert blows. These people are "deep shelter conscious". They are drab, dreary, and look infinitely sad—standing in the queues for their places, for which they have tickets. Squatting on the metal treads of narrow stairs, there to hunch up asleep all night. Stretched out in a bunk, with electric trains swishing and roaring past every few minutes.

To supper with Noel Coward and Clemence Dane.[211] She is portly and motherly, but of immense versatility—her sculpture and painting being remarkably talented.

Saturday April 26th

"Times", which is doing me well, publishes my Anzac speech verbatim on the cable page—an honour hitherto reserved for Winston.

Drive down to Churt[212] to lunch with Lloyd George, who is as clear headed as ever, and has some shrewd things to say about Cabinet organisation, Winston's leadership, and the like. We found we had many ideas in common, much as follows—

---

208   Field-Marshal Lord Birdwood, first commander of the Australian and New Zealand contingents in the First World War and commander of the Australian Army Corps at its formation in 1917.

209   Field-Marshal Lord Milne.

210   By Anzac Day news of the disastrous defeat and losses of Australians and New Zealanders in Greece was fully out. In his address at the lunch Menzies declared that 'we regret nothing'. It was a moral duty to come to Greece's aid and in the process it was shown 'that the sons of Anzacs are fit to be called sons, and to become the fathers, of the race they are fighting for'. *The Times*, 26 April 1941.

211   Clemence Dane (Winifred Ashton), playwright and novelist, was a lifelong friend of Coward's and had taught him painting.

212   Shortly before leaving office Lloyd George had built a house and set up a 600 acre farm at Churt, in Surrey, and had lived there since 1932.

1. Winston is acting as the master strategist, without qualification and without really forceful chiefs of staff to guide him.

2. Dill has ability, but is as timid as a hare.

3. There is no War Cabinet, since W.C. deals with conduct of the war himself, by "directives" &c and his Ministers just concur.

4. Beaverbrook might have some influence, but he is up to the neck in the detail of aircraft construction, and simply has no time for general study and appreciation. No War Cabinet Minister here should have anything to attend to except War Cabinet.

5. War Cabinet should meet every morning. This week, this crucial and anxious week, it has met twice for an hour and $1\frac{1}{2}$ hours respectively!

6. Winston should be at the helm, instead of touring the bombed areas, as he has been doing most of this week. Let the King & Queen do this. In any case they do it much better.

7. More food could be grown in this country, but there is nobody finally responsible for comprehensive policy, which must include food, agriculture, fisheries, and so on. Many ministers, many opinions. Same with <u>shipping</u>. M/Shipping attends to the fag end e.g. charter parties, Admiralty builds and mends ships, Labour controls labour, Transport the getting of the goods off the wharves, Supply what can be carried on the ships &c &c.

In brief, Churchill is a bad organiser.

8. A non-executive War Cabinet <u>must</u> contain a Dominions man, for the Dominions type of mind is essential.

9. The problem of a couple of good men to prop up Churchill is acute. He is not interested in finance, economics, or agriculture, and ignores the debates on all three. He loves war and spends hours with the maps and charts, working out fresh combinations. He has aggression without knowledge or at any rate without any love for inconvenient knowledge. His advisers are presumed to have knowledge but haven't enough aggression to convey it to Churchill.

10. Foreign policy is deplorable—eg Japan. We never have ideas, and we never beat Germany to it. Alex Cadogan is a dull dog, if not actually a dead dog.

11. Eden has not trained on, and John Anderson is a bureaucrat par excellence—no imagination, or sweep, or fire.

L.G. frankly does not see how we win the war though he agrees we will not lose it. But he points out that Germany has a couple of million skilled workers now available in Italy, France and Czecho Slovakia, who can, even if not trusted to make aircraft, make other things such as M/T and so relieve the pressure on Germany. They <u>must</u> work, if they are to live. Why, then, he says, should we think that USA and UK can outbuild Hitler? And if we do, why does that end the matter? Hitler has had a vast superiority of bombers, both in numbers and place, but, though destruction here is terrific, he has not destroyed us or deterred us! L.G. plainly thinks we are wishfully thinking. But L.G. was equally indeterminate on the question "If there is a stalemate and a negotiated peace, what next?"

He rates Hitler's ability very high, and comes back to the melancholy truth that the Germans in their hearts like us much more than the French ever did.

Sunday April 27th

A wise article by General Fuller in the "Sunday Pictorial".[213]

Little news from Greece, but 13 000 men got away to Crete on Friday night, and so there are hopes of a decent percentage of evacuation. It is a terrible anxiety.

Interesting talk with Winant. We both think news to America badly handled—most stuff going to USA is of German origin, in spite of overwhelming friendliness of American journals and journalists.

What about a joint supply board UK, USA, and Dominions, seeing that Lease-Lend Bill[214] has brought America openly into the picture?

Monday April 28th

Lunch with Lord Trenchard at Brooks's. A little deaf, but mentally active. Most unhappy about policy. Against bombing in France, because the bombs that miss kill Frenchmen, whereas the ones that miss in Germany kill Germans. Would send even single aircraft over as many German towns as possible. Believes that Germans do not take this kind of thing as well as we do.

War Cabinet. Winston says "We will lose only 5000 in Greece". We will in fact lose at least 15000. W. is a great man, but he is more addicted to wishful thinking every day. Acute exchanges on news. I say that propaganda bad—best propaganda news, especially in Australia and U.S.A. But British Services are against news. In the Greek campaign "our retirement is continuing"! But German High Command puts out half a column! American press anxious to help but no material. W.C. is proud of his handling of Roosevelt, and rightly so. But he forgets the American people and Congress—so do most of his colleagues. As usual, Beaverbrook supports me, but "the rest is silence", apart from Duff Cooper, who surprisingly, backs me hard.

Dine the press-men, and hear an interesting symposium of views on the war and its conduct.

---

213   Major-General J.F.C. Fuller, 'Our Vital Hour', *Sunday Pictorial*, 27 April 1941. Menzies retained a clipping of this article with his 1941 Diary. Fuller was a retired First World War general and a war historian.

214   The Lend-Lease Act had been passed by Congress in March 1941.

Tuesday April 29th

See Kim Mackay, and then Reggie Bessemer Clark, whiskered and solemn, enquiring anxiously after Elaine. Looks well and plainly and naturally does not want Elaine and the child here at a time like this.

Lunch with W.S. Robinson, who is very friendly.

Send off revised speeches to publishers, Longman's Green, who will now make an offer.

Meet one Hiros,[215] of Press Wireless of America, who is interesting on Germany & France after the collapse of France. Satisfied that as time goes on French hate the Germans more and more.

Also meet Ian Hay (Beith)[216] who has a face like a greyhound, and, like so many professional humourists, has no brightness in conversation.

Then to Defence Committee to discuss "what next" if Egypt falls. The answer is a lemon i.e. Winston says "Let us keep our minds on <u>victory</u>". I argue a great deal and nobody else says anything!

I am 2 years Prime Minister today!

Wednesday April 30th

Clearing up. Whenever we leave, we leave in a hurry. Queer trait in human nature! Great argument in War Cabinet. I protest against W.C. deciding what advice to offer USA regarding moving Pacific fleet (or a real section of it) to the Atlantic, <u>without</u> reference to Australia, though I was in London!

I was too late after flying to Swansea via Cardiff, to receive the freedom of Swansea. Last night Cardiff visited by land mines and I see the smoking results!

Picturesque but in some ways horrible day.

Thursday & Friday May 1 & 2

Confusion and hurry. Show films to Australia House. Long talk with Winston regarding the help he needs in Cabinet. Long talk Beaverbrook, who is afraid of his health—approves of me, and thinks absurd that I should go back to Australia! I am desperately afraid of the future in Great Britain.[217]

---

215 Handwriting unclear.

216 Major-General John Hay Beith, pseudonym Ian Hay, was a novelist and playwright probably best remembered for his first novel *Pip*. He was also Director of Public Relations at the War Office.

217 Menzies was present at the War Cabinet meeting on 1 May and was farewelled effusively by Churchill, who declared that Menzies 'had won an outstanding place in the esteem of the British people, and would take back to Australia the admiration and affection of all'. In reply the visitor thanked British Ministers for 'their courtesy and kindness. The experience and knowledge which he had gained during his visit would be of the utmost value to him.' War Cabinet, 1 May 1941, PRO CAB 65/18/103.

3 – 24 May

Leaving Bristol by DC3 on 3 May, Menzies travels uneventfully to Lisbon, then is delayed there awaiting his Clipper flight to America. That gives him the opportunity of seeing a bull-fight, of talking with the Portuguese dictator, Salazar, and of generally enjoying Lisbon's sun and colour. Flying then by the Azores he lands at La Guardia airport, New York, on 6 May, to be met by Richard Casey, the Australian Ambassador and an old parliamentary colleague of Menzies. Next day he flies to Canada, where as the guest of the Prime Minister, Mackenzie King, he addresses Parliament, receives a triumphant reception, and briefs the Canadian Cabinet on the British War Cabinet's workings. Back in the United States by 9 May, he meets leading local politicians and jurists, talks to Roosevelt, and writes and speaks eloquently on the great question of the moment: the delicate position of the United States, being at once not formally in the war, and yet the crucial source of succour for Great Britain. On 16 and 17 May Menzies flies across the American continent and calls briefly at Los Angeles before the Pacific 'hop' via Honolulu and New Caledonia to New Zealand. In Auckland on 23 May he is given a State Dinner at Government House and a Civic Reception at the Town Hall. The following day he flies over the Tasman, through clouds and west winds, to a homecoming whose prospect does not fill him with pleasure.

<u>Saturday May 3rd</u>

Bristol to Lisbon by land plane—DC3—good and luckily uneventful journey of 6½ hours. Lisbon quite lovely, colour, iron work, wall tiles—stay at Campbell's—Embassy. He speaks highly of Peter & Elizabeth Garran.[1]

<u>Sunday May 4th</u> Clipper postponed a day. Sunny day: Lisbon—Estoril—Bull fight a spectacle of colour, swank and cruelty, worth seeing once.

Call on Dr Salazar, the Prime Minister—practically dictator. Very sincere and earnest. Was a professor and still is at heart. Very little public contact—a sincere Christian. Runs all out of revenue—no loans internal or external!

---

1   Isham Peter Garran, Second Secretary at the British Embassy in Lisbon, was born in Melbourne, the son of Sir Robert Garran, a former Solicitor-General and one of the framers of the Australian Constitution.

The Portuguese won't fight and why should they! I hope we don't encourage them too much on the strength of Winston's recollection of the hues of Torres Vedras.

Plenty of sun and colour—the tiles on the walls—the women carrying their large flat fish baskets on their heads.

Arthur Yencken present, looking fitter and younger than ever. Sends greetings to Joyce. We could I think get him to organise & direct our External Affairs Dept for a couple of years, seconded from F.O.

<u>Monday May 5th</u> Leave by Clipper "Dixie Clipper". Good pilot and roomy plane, but seats fixed and sleeping bunks excruciating—with iron rod pressing the rib. Fellow passengers include Wilfrid Greene[2] and A.L. Goodhart.[3]

Call at Horta, in Azores. Damp, mountainous, blotches on walls, and a long-anchored German merchant ship in harbour. Portuguese. We ought to take these islands before the Germans do.

Off through the night.

<u>Tuesday May 6th</u>

Head winds all way. Arrive Bermuda—many houses and little land. Governor General Barnard who talks of Sir Wm Glasgow.[4] A dozen or so of PBY's,[5] being tuned before their 3000 mile hop to England.

Breakfast and away to La Guardia 'drome, out of New York. A Douglas arrives or departs every 4 minutes![6]

Met by Caseys, then to Ritz-Carlton for dinner. Ring up Pat and Ken,[7] & go to bed late, when so overtired that make false awakening & arise at 3 a.m.!

<u>Wednesday May 7th</u> Fly, per Douglas Bomber, with Goble[8] (full of grievances re rank and pay) to Ottawa. Met by McKenzie King and inspect and address some Australian air trainees. Then press interviews, in which I sense that King is more criticised in Canada than I am in Australia. But, per contra, he has a

---

2	Sir Wilfrid Arthur Greene, KC, Master of the Rolls.
3	Arthur Lehman Goodhart, American academic lawyer and Anglophile, Professor of Jurisprudence at Oxford University.
4	Major-General Sir T. William Glasgow, Australian High Commissioner in Canada.
5	PBY—the Consolidated Catalina, a US Navy patrol flying boat.
6	On arrival, Menzies told the press: 'The United States can do a great service to humanity ... if she wants to ... You are not being asked to make a donation to a deserving charity. You are being asked to defend your own way of life.' *New York Times*, 7 May 1941.
7	Kenneth Menzies, his eldest son, then aged nineteen.
8	Air Vice-Marshal Stanley Jones Goble, Australian Liaison Officer for the Empire Air Training Scheme in Canada.

loyal following. They stick to their leaders here. He has been P.M. 14 years and Liberal leader 23!

Address 800 members of Canadian Club at Chateau Laurier on the war and giving all to win it.[9] Terrific reception and P.M. invites me to attend House at 3 pm to address members in the Chamber. This done. A quite unique affair, save that Viviani and Balfour had done it years ago. Terrific enthusiasm, members applauding by beating on the tables.

Ottawa looking green & lovely—with water everywhere—the Athlones (Princess Alice)[10] are my hosts & are charming. Glasgow's house a bargain (15,000 dols)—very roomy & well furnished.

Attend War Committee of Cabinet and give the inside story of Whitehall. Dine at Country Club with Cabinet &c. Speak and show films. Everybody very friendly & responsive, as are the press. A prophet and his own country!

Go to bed dog tired, for I have today made 5 speeches after having 5 hours sleep in about 3 days. What junketings travelling ministers have!

<u>Thursday May 8th</u>   Breakfast with Glasgow & Malcolm Macdonald, who is concerned about Australia's outlook. His actual words "They never know when they have a great P.M., and they never back him". Subject to the fact that I am not great at all, he is right. We are parochial, jealous and ungenerous to those who serve us. The Sydney taint!

King sees me off, also Power[11] (Air) and Ralston[12] (Munitions).

Rail to Toronto, where pick up Tim Clapp, who comes with me as far as Buffalo. There I change trains and go off to Washington. Canada looking superbly green and well watered.

King feels he has done well in

(a) Keeping unity

(b) Keeping USA onside, he being a close personal friend of Roosevelt.

As to (a), he seems right, for the French Canadians (esp. Cardinal Villeneuve)[13] are OK. But he is not a war leader, possesses no <u>burning</u> zeal for the cause, and is a politican who possibly prefers to lead from behind. All the

---

9   'All I want to say is to repeat to you what I say to myself. Nothing matters except that we should so act now that when the war is over we shall live in a free world, in the kind of world in which we want to live.' *Sydney Morning Herald*, 9 May 1941.

10   Lord Athlone, Governor-General of Canada, and his wife Princess Alice.

11   Charles Gavan ('Chubby') Power, lawyer and politician, was Minister of National Defence for Air.

12   Colonel James Layton Ralston, a battalion commander in the First World War, was twice Minister of National Defence, from 1926 to 1930 and from 1940.

13   Cardinal Jean-Marie-Rodrigue Villeneuve, Roman Catholic Archbishop of Quebec since 1933.

same, he pleasantly surprised me and, after (I was told) not really wanting me to come to Canada, he could not have been more pleasant and co-operative.

Among the French Canadians, I liked Lapointe[14] (Justice Minister) who is a rugged and amusing character, and a really great speaker. By the way, my own speech to the Commons is in the Canadian Hansard.

Friday May 9th

Washington. Noticeably grown since I last saw it 6 years ago. The full fresh green of spring on the trees, the houses set in a deep verdure. It is quite lovely.

Go to see Cordell Hull,[15] who is very fit. Still a bit wordy, but absolutely sound on the war. Indeed, I gather that the whole Cabinet would come into the war tomorrow if Roosevelt would say the word. But he hangs back, preferring an "incident" (e.g. as a result of the Atlantic patrol) to a formal declaration.

Hull hopes we will not make the peace errors we did last time. I agree & suggest that joint executive control of supplies by U.S.A., U.K. and Dominions during the war would be good training for post-war co-operation, & would do much to avoid what I fear—that after the war the casting up of the Lease-lend transactions may give rise to bitterness, misunderstanding and recrimination.

Lunch at Legation—a perfect place—to be purchased (if we will) for $200 000! The price, on comparison locally, is correct. In Australia it would cost about £20 000!

Press interview—successful—the questions are bowled on the wicket, but I keep my right foot from dragging over the crease. The line here, is not so much "help us" as "help yourselves. This is your fight". Not the politics of Europe; but the politics of common humanity!

At dinner, after, interesting talk about Pacific, naval dispositions, &c. Dr Hornbeck[16] very good, as also Admiral Danckwerts of R.N.[17] Dean Atcheson,[18] of State Dept, friendly but confused. Famous Harry Hopkins[19] a great disappointment—a sort of gangling yokel. Stimson[20] old & quiet.

---

14   Ernest Lapointe, Minister of Justice, 1924–30 and from 1935, was recognised as Mackenzie King's Quebec lieutenant and his most influential adviser.

15   Cordell Hull, Secretary of State, now aged seventy but still Roosevelt's right-hand man.

16   Dr Stanley Hornbeck, Adviser on Political Relations, Department of State.

17   Rear-Admiral Victor Hilary Danckwerts was a member of the British delegation to the Anglo-American talks in Washington.

18   Dean Acheson, Assistant Secretary of State.

19   Harry Lloyd Hopkins, social worker, administrator and diplomat, was personal adviser to Roosevelt and the chief architect of the lend-lease program.

20   Henry Lewis Stimson, Secretary for War and a former Governor-General of the Philippines.

Justice Murphy[21] a most pro-British Irishman, pleased with my analysis of the Irish situation.

Saturday May 10th

Long talk with leading columnists, especially Walter Lippman[22] of N.Y. Times, who tells me afterwards that my statements here are quite the best for the American psychology.

[NB Both in America & London, our people complain that cables are not answered, or that there are dangerous delays and opportunities missed. My own experience (+ Tim Clapp & Dick Casey) bears this out. We must have a cable supervisor who follows up cables. Sees that they are promptly answered!]

Sunday May 11th } Washington. Speak to the Press Club & have
Monday May 12th } great reception. See President, in <u>bed</u>.

Tuesday May 13th } New York. Speak to Nat Dfce C'tee (sort of
Wed May 14th } Chatham House) at Dinner, do a Broadcast, and
speak at Businessmen's luncheon Down Town Ass[n].

Thursday May 15th Chicago. Speak at Nat Dfce C'tee to 1500 people
(& broadcast), including Rev. Ossy McCall:[23]
Looks like Colin Traviller.

General Reflections

General American sentiment is on our side, but the moral arguments of cowardice and short-range self-interest are being directed by Hoover,[24] Wheeler[25] Lindbergh[26] & Co to the mothers and possible draftees! The slogan "help Britain" is most imperfect—should be "help ourselves". That has been my own theme—"This is <u>your</u> struggle as well as ours, and you must organise your material resources accordingly."

---

21   Justice Frank Murphy, former Attorney-General, 1939–40, and US Supreme Court Justice.

22   Walter Lippmann, author and influential editorial writer, was also an army military intelligence officer.

23   Oswald Walter Samuel McCall, an Australian-born clergyman then ministering in Chicago, was also a popular writer and broadcaster.

24   Herbert Hoover, former President of the United States, now a staunch opponent of American involvement in the war.

25   Senator Burton Kendall Wheeler, isolationist leader in the US Senate.

26   Charles A. Lindbergh, the famous aviator, prominent isolationist broadcaster and executive committee member of the America First Movement.

Menzies' Dixie Clipper arrives at La Guardia airport, New York, and he addresses the United States press. (top—Menzies Papers; below—AWM 7423)

A serious Menzies briefs US journalists on his experiences of wartime Britain. (Menzies Papers)

Menzies attends a special conference of the War Committee of the Canadian Cabinet.
(Menzies Papers)

Public opinion has gone as far as it can without a lead by the President, whose delay becomes disturbing. Public opinion is creative only up to a point. After that it must be created by decision and action. Roosevelt could decide tomorrow to convoy, and the people would back him. He could probably decide not to, and the people would back him.

Roosevelt was in bed recovering from a touch of gastritis. He looks older and more tired, but my hour with him, with fair give and take of conversation, was most vigorous. He (and Hull) agreed that we all ought to tell Japan where she gets off, but each of them stops short of actually instructing the USA Ambassador to do so. But, I am left in no doubt (without words) that America will not stand by & see Australia attacked. I plead for reality about N.E.I. and Singapore.

Don't think Pacific will be denuded of USA naval forces.

R. is a little jealous of Winston's place in the centre of the picture. I tell him they should have a meeting.

R. is not an organiser—very like Winston—and co-ordination of effort is not conspicuous.

Hull is loquacious but very sound and clear-minded about the war—much clearer than many of the officers of his department. He, & all the leading ministers, are for war and nothing less. But the President, trained under Woodrow Wilson in the last war, waits for an incident, which would in one blow get the USA into war and get R. out of his foolish election pledges that "I will keep you out of war". Henry Wallace, Vice President, is a dreamer and a philosopher with a quiet and engaging personality, and a passion for throwing boomerangs!

Senator George,[27] Chairman of the Senate Foreign Rel. C'tee, a fine solid man whom R. tried to push out a few years ago, but who now is a trusty supporter of both R. and ours. Tall, solid, grey, glasses, the perfect type of Senator.

Sol Bloom,[28] Chairman of Reps For. Rel. C'tee, is a short, dark, comedian. Great fun, a great supporter. He wrote "You are the honeysuckle" &c &c, and knows the Albert[29] people in Sydney very well.

This is the only country in the world where they will pay to hear you speak. A leading Senator will get 750 dollars for an appearance. Casey has been paid (for some charity) up to 250 dollars! I must come back!

---

27 Senator Walter Franklin George, Judge, US Senator and Chairman of the Senate Foreign Relations Committee since 1940.

28 Sol Bloom's background was in newspapers, theatre and music publishing.

29 The Albert family, a prominent Sydney firm of music retailers and publishers.

Sumner Welles[30] tall, solemn, a good dome of a head, but without colour or vivacity!

Dean Atcheson (N°·2 to Hull) is able but confused. But he at least sees that action of some kind is necessary to get American policy "off centre"!

Dr. Hornbeck solid and a little heavy, but 100% sound on Singapore and the Far East. We were in complete agreement.

Justice Felix Frankfurter[31]—small, dapper, alive, glasses, was a great teacher at Harvard, and has a great and deserved following. I fall for him at once. The true Liberal with no cant or "isms". Great admiration for Evatt's ability, but a little disillusioned about his character.

C.E. Hughes, C.J.[32] a little like Joe Cook in appearance—breezy, clear and youthful Yankee style.

Stimson, Secretary for War. Fine old house and fine old man. A little deaf, and a little comfortable about the Pacific, but otherwise sound and a fine influence (A Republican, like Knox).[33]

Each State is allowed 2 statues of its great men in the Hall of Fame at the Capitol. Louisiana has just erected one to Huey Long![34] This induces sober reflections.

Eugene Meyer,[35] of the "Washington Post", cables Churchill to say that my speeches are best yet made in USA on the war, and that I should be invited to stay in USA for a couple of weeks!

Admiral Stark, Chief of Naval Staff, is an alert, white headed man, but came up on ordnance side and has no great ideas on strategy. General Marshall, Chief of the Army, is tall, very able & clear headed, and impressed me more than any general I met in England. Tells a terrible story about how the USA forces were cut down—Army to 116,000 in 1939, and Air Force (controlled by army in USA) to 57 planes! Australians who groan at me should come here & have a look see. The President is still the only "minister" responsible for munitions!

The Casey's are a very great success, but once more I am embarrassed. Dick asks for (a) the C.H.[36]

---

30   Sumner Welles, US Under-Secretary of State. In February–March 1940, as the personal representative of President Roosevelt, he had visited heads of government in Italy, Germany, France and England, as well as Pope Pius XII.

31   Justice Felix Frankfurter, academic lawyer and teacher, had been Associate Justice of the United States Supreme Court since 1939.

32   Charles Evans Hughes, Chief Justice of the United States Supreme Court.

33   Colonel W. Franklin Knox, Secretary of the US Navy.

34   Huey Long, the flamboyant, demagogic and ruthlessly autocratic Governor of Louisiana from 1928 until he was assassinated in 1935.

35   Eugene Meyer, influential publisher and editor of the *Washington Post*.

36   Companion of Honour.

(b) a roving commission to cover U.K. and Middle East!!! He asks for each in Maie's presence! He is the bitterest disappointment of my life. Is quite plainly on the make. Moral, in politics, trust nobody!

McCloy[37]—ordnance—Caruja[38]—very clear headed.

Leon Henderson[39]—a rough diamond who looks like Geo Mooney—controls prices, is well regarded as an economist. Keynes is in touch with him. General "Happy" Arnold runs the Air Force but does not seem first class.

Senator Pepper[40]—an ugly fellow, but a real "smash & grab" supporter of war. Has a dangerous wife, but agreeable.

In N.Y., Al Smith,[41] Chairman took me up Empire State Building & pointed to the Bronx where he was born. He is a museum piece "Toity-toid Street".

Mayor La Guardia[42] is a dynamic little man, and I found him good. La Guardia airfield is his pride, and it well might be.

F.B. Clapp[43]

Dorabi[44]

L.R. McGregor[45]

J.W. Davis, former Ambassador.[46]

Long talk with <u>Donovan</u>, who is even better than I thought. I would like to see him in the joint War Cabinet. Fine apartment looking over the East River. <u>Police guards.</u>

J.P. Morgan,[47] T.W. Lamont[48]

37	John J. McCloy, Assistant Secretary of War.
38	Handwriting unclear.
39	Leon Henderson, economist and government adviser, directed the Price Administration and Supply Allocation.
40	Claude Denson Pepper, lawyer and US Senator.
41	Alfred Emanuel ('Al') Smith had been four times Democratic Governor of New York and was the first Roman Catholic to run for the presidency. By 1940, however, he had become a Republican supporter.
42	Fiorello Henry ('The Little Flower') La Guardia, a flyer in the First World War, was in his third term as Mayor of New York City.
43	Francis B. Clapp, Australian General Manager of General Electric, and Director of Purchases for the Commonwealth Government in New York and Washington.
44	Handwriting unclear.
45	Lewis R. Macgregor, Australian Trade Commissioner in the US, held a reception for Menzies at the Ritz-Carlton on the previous Tuesday.
46	John William Davis, Chairman of the Council of Foreign Relations and a former presidential candidate, had been US Ambassador in London, 1918–21.
47	John Pierpont Morgan was the head of the J.P. Morgan bank.
48	Thomas William Lamont, international financier, had helped to organise the Committee to Defend America by Aiding the Allies. He was Chairman of the executive committee of the J.P. Morgan bank.

Mayor Kelly[49] of Chicago

Fri. May 16th   The strange deserts of Wyoming, Utah, with snow-clad mountains beyond.

<u>Saturday May 17th</u>   Los Angeles. New, sprawling. O'Connor, our publicity man. Reminds me of   [50] in London—curiously wordy. Good public buildings. "Hall of Justice" has upper three floors used as County Jail—a room with a view!

Off on overnight hop from San Pedro to Honolulu—2600 miles. A smooth journey & early arrival among the warships at Pearl Harbour. Then to Royal Hawaiian. Riot of colour. Waikiki beach very colourful, & good crowd (including many white-clad sailors) though it is between seasons.

Put in busy day dictating stuff to a borrowed stenographer. Tomorrow early to Canton Island, on the Equator, where I shall imitate a Porterhouse steak.

<u>Monday May 19th</u>   I was right. Canton Island is a coral atoll, greatest height above water level 12 feet. Very good rest house of Pan American, with beach and engineering services. There is one original inhabitant, the British Resident, who lives in a bark hut with a native wife, and runs the wireless station.

North bound clipper arrives in the dark and makes a fine landing— watching it was an eerie experience. On board were (inter alia) Gordon Coates[51] of N.Z. and Angus Mitchell,[52] off to some Rotary Conference in America! The child is indeed father of the man.

A sweaty night, but made tolerable that 10 000 feet up in the air (as I discovered today crossing the Equator) it can be and is most pleasantly cold. Indeed, flying today I did hours of writing and preparation for my Australian landfall.

<u>Tuesday May 20th</u>   which, because we cross the International Date Line (oh sacred mystery) is also

<u>Wednesday May 21st</u>

Beautifully cool up above, after a start delayed from 5 to 5.30 by some temporary shortage in the oil pressure. Do a good deal of writing, in

---

49   Edward Joseph Kelly, political boss and Mayor of Chicago, had spearheaded Roosevelt's campaign in 1940.

50   Menzies has left a space here.

51   Joseph Gordon Coates, Prime Minister of New Zealand, 1925–28, and a member of the New Zealand War Cabinet since 1940.

52   Angus Mitchell, former President of the Rotary Club of Melbourne, and a director of Rotary International since 1937.

preparation for Australian arrival, where I will be expected to hand out five accounts of everything!

Arrive at New Caledonia—a quite rugged and beautiful country, with a sort of mauve flush on the jagged hills quite reminiscent of Scotland.

At Noumea met by Ballard,[53] Governor-General Brunot,[54] Governor Sautot[55] and a guard of honour. Across to main landing stage, where a terrific reception by entire population headed by M. le Maire, who reads an address of welcome. I air a few halting words of French. Present, an English group and an Australian group—hundreds of school children. "Vive Menzies" say they. "Vive la France libre" says I. Dine at Government House, where Brunot, who has no English, explained the Darlan Laval[56] type of mind as essentially Fascist. So hostile to the Front Populaire and so out for <u>order</u> that they prefer <u>order</u> under Germany to disorder, as they see it, under democracy. Thus it appears that Fascism or Nazism conquered France before the war began!

Sleep on anchored yacht "Southern Seas" in Noumea Harbour.

<u>Thursday May 22nd</u>   To Auckland via Norfolk Island. Met by Nash[57] & Sullivan,[58] stay with Newalls[59] (good company and a cheerful young family) at Government House. State Dinner, where Nash, proposing me, speaks for 75 minutes. A wordy and platitudinous fellow but quite shrewd in detailed discussion. Les[60] and Margaret looking well. Have not seen Les for 3 years. He is popular here.

<u>Friday May 23rd</u>

Civic Reception at Town Hall, where thousands turn up and give me a rousing reception. Savage's Tomb.[61] Housing Schemes (very costly & ∴ high rent).

---

53   Bertram C. Ballard, Australian Official Representative in New Caledonia.

54   Commandant Richard Brunot, representative of de Gaulle on a special mission to French Oceania in April 1941.

55   Henri Camille Sautot, appointed temporary Governor, Free New Caledonia, in September 1940 by de Gaulle.

56   Pierre Laval, Marshal Pétain's chief minister, was the most outspokenly pro-German member of the Vichy Government. His arrogance and over-readiness to collaborate caused Pétain to dismiss him in December 1940 and appoint Admiral François Darlan, former Commander-in-Chief of the French Navy and Minister of Marine, and another leading appeaser of the Germans, in his stead.

57   Walter Nash, the Minister of Finance and Deputy Prime Minister of New Zealand, was Acting Prime Minister at the time.

58   Daniel G. Sullivan, Minister of Supply and Munitions.

59   Sir Cyril Newall, former Chief of the Air Staff, was Governor-General of New Zealand.

60   James Leslie ('Les') Menzies, Menzies' eldest brother, was the Acting Trade Commissioner to New Zealand.

61   Menzies laid a wreath on the tomb of the former Prime Minister of New Zealand, Michael Joseph Savage, at Bastion Point.

Dine at G.H. & show films—the later ones are very good indeed.

A sick feeling of repugnance and apprehension grows in me as I near Australia. If only I could creep in quietly into the bosom of the family, and rest there.

Saturday May 24th

Clouds & west winds over Tasman. The hour approaches!

EPILOGUE

'A sick feeling of repugnance and apprehension grows in me as I near Australia. If only I could creep in quietly into the bosom of the family and rest there.' These, the near-final words of the Diary, have been quoted *ad nauseam*, out of context and often even without the second sentence about family, by writers anxious to show that Menzies was in some way not a true Australian, but in fact a man who had contempt for, or at the very least disliked, his own country, and longed to be an Englishman, living in England. To anyone who reads the whole Diary and carefully follows its author's experiences and changing moods, this interpretation of two sentences at the end can only be considered absurd, indeed mischievous. Throughout the Diary a dominant theme is in fact *pride* in the achievements of Australia in the war—'Australia,' Menzies says, 'is ace high'[1]— and, while he is full of admiration for the courage of the British people in the face of their sufferings, he can be scathing about their leaders' blunders, especially when the fate of Australians is involved. He wants Australian troops to be commanded by Australians, and fiercely deplores in the War Cabinet any British initiative which affects Australian interests but which is taken without consultation. The care to separate Australia as independent partner, rather than Imperial pawn, in the war effort is a constant in his public speeches. As he finally left London in May 1941 *The Times* presented Menzies with a valedictory editorial which underlined this point, observing that 'his presence here, his share in council, and the grace and force of a whole series of eloquent speeches have made a very real contribution to the common cause at a time when the Empire is facing a stern trial ... He has ... made it unmistakably plain to the world that Australia is with us to the last.'[2] A man who in his public utterances could create such a clear impression of his country's separate and robust identity is scarcely likely at the same time to be a despiser of that country. Nor is one who in the privacy of his own room records the feelings of homesickness which are to be found in this Diary.

What then could have been the cause of the 'sick feeling of repugnance and apprehension'? Sheer fatigue at the end of a gruelling few months has in the first place to be noted as an essential element in Menzies' condition at this time. He notes his weariness at various points in the Diary, and all who met him at the

---

1   Menzies 1941 Diary, 5 March.
2   *The Times*, 5 May 1941.

Rose Bay terminal in Sydney on the morning of 24 May remarked on his drawn appearance: one reporter described him as 'tired and grim';[3] more colourfully, Arthur Fadden, the Acting Prime Minister, later wrote that Menzies seemed to him 'about as happy as a sailor on a horse'.[4] Before his arrival a group of Menzies' oldest and closest Melbourne political friends, headed by Ferdinand Wright and Staniforth Ricketson, had conferred with his wife and his brother Frank and worked out a program of public meetings for him to address, but this had to be modified when the Prime Minister made it clear to Mrs Menzies that he would urgently need rest.[5] As the flying boat crossed the Tasman Menzies recapitulated and set down, either through his secretary or Shedden, an outline of the trip and the work it had involved. It had been carried out by 'the smallest party ever to have left Australia on a mission of such wide scope'. In retrospect Menzies felt the party too small: the work had been such as to impose a great strain on them all, and he frankly admitted to himself that he could never have coped without the sanity and hard work of his four companions. In four months he had travelled 42 000 miles, 36 000 of them by air. Travel to and from Britain had occupied thirty-four days, and the party had brought home official papers weighing a total of 230 pounds. Menzies had given ninety speeches and broadcasts, had conferences with officials at all stopping places on his way to Britain and, beside his numerous public appearances as speaker once he got there, had regularly attended the War Cabinet and had numerous meetings with ministers and officials on special subjects.[6]

It was not only that all this work had been in itself so tiring. Menzies knew that on his return he would be expected to report extensively on it. 'Do a good deal of writing, in preparation for Australian arrival,' he records, 'where I will be expected to hand out five accounts of everything!' That was on 21 May, as he flew over the Pacific. Three days later, when compiling notes on the trip, Menzies' secretary added a few lines on what was ahead: 'There will be no "let up" for the P.M. on arrival in Australia as several weeks will be necessary to deal with his discussions abroad. He plans to do this by a session of Parliament, and meetings of the Cabinet, War Cabinet and the Advisory War Council. He will also make several public addresses and broadcasts.'[7] For a tired man who, despite a usual veneer of self-confidence, sometimes found public appearances draining, all this was not a comfortable prospect.

---

3   *Sydney Morning Herald*, 26 May 1941.

4   Arthur Fadden, *They Called Me Artie* (Brisbane, 1969), p. 60.

5   Wright to Menzies, 15 May 1941, F.H. Wright Papers, National Library of Australia MS 8119/2/15.

6   'The Prime Minister's Trip Abroad', 24 May 1941, Menzies Family Papers.

7   Ibid.

Pat Menzies with her husband on his arrival home at Rose Bay Flying Boat Base, before they disappear for a brief rest. (Australasian, 31 May 1941)

Back home again, Menzies shows his wife Pat, daughter Heather and son Ken a bomb splinter picked up in a London street. (Australasian, 7 June 1941)

But what, above all, raised apprehension was the political situation to which Menzies was returning. Still in a minority, held in power only by a couple of Independents, his Government was as precarious as ever. Just as he arrived, a by-election for a South Australian seat, Boothby, was in progress, with inevitable party competition. Fresh from a Britain in which party differences were muted through a national government, an agitated Menzies depicted the by-election, and other real or imagined signs of party division in Australia, as insufferable. As he stepped onto the landing at Rose Bay he told an impromptu press conference that it was 'a diabolical thing that anybody should have to come back and play politics, however clean and however friendly, at a time like this'. In Britain he had learned the lesson of unity: there all parties were represented in a real War Cabinet; there the bombs fell equally on Buckingham Palace and the slums near the docks. But 'all the time I was in London the Australian cables would almost continually report alleged political dissensions, rumours of political difficulties, and ill-informed criticisms which added tremendously to the burden which I was endeavouring to carry'.[8] That was highly unfair to John Curtin and some other senior members of the Labor Party, who had shown marked courtesy and cooperation in the Government's war measures, and they hastened to say so. Menzies' remarks did, however, accurately apply to some members of the Labor Party, the most notable of whom was H.V. Evatt, who were anxious for office and pressed for the Government's overthrow.[9] Menzies sensed danger from this quarter; but it was as nothing to the threat to his position from within his own nominal following. That, undoubtedly, was what most of all induced a 'sick feeling of repugnance' and the wistful, because impossible, wish that the cup could pass from him, and that he might creep quietly into the bosom of his family.

During her husband's absence abroad Pat Menzies correctly sensed that plots against his leadership were being hatched and twice in vain urged him to hurry home. Part of the danger clearly came from his partner in the Coalition, the Country Party, elements of which had always been suspicious of Menzies.

---

8 *Sydney Morning Herald*, 26 May 1941.

9 Among the abundant evidence for this, the Diary of H.E. Boote, editor of the *Worker*, offers some of the most colourful. At this time Boote saw much of Evatt: beside party connections, both were on the Board of the New South Wales Public Library. In January 1941 Boote recorded that 'Evatt, I can see, is passionately desirous of office. This colours all he says.' During Menzies' absence Evatt tried to engineer a favourable Labor response to the Prime Minister's calls for a national, all-party government, and was the only Labor member present at the wharf when Menzies arrived at Rose Bay on 24 May. But as the possibility of a national government receded, Evatt decided that Labor should 'resolutely strive to throw the Menzies Government out, and take its place'. That meant railing at the 'lack of militancy' shown by Curtin and the other senior party men, Chifley and Scullin. H.E. Boote Papers, National Library of Australia MS 2070/2/2. We are grateful to Dr Frank Farrell for drawing our attention to this document.

From his experience as a politician in Victoria the latter had brought a half-hidden but deep-seated distaste for Country parties as predatory sectional groups. Earle Page, the Country Party's former leader, frankly remained a personal enemy. It was rumoured among Menzies' supporters that Arthur Fadden, Page's successor and Menzies' Deputy Prime Minister, would also be secretly happy to see Menzies go. Percy Spender, one of Menzies' UAP ministers, got wind of a possible Country Party plot to remove Menzies and wrote a letter to intercept him in New Zealand, to warn him that 'his political grave was being dug'.[10] Within the UAP itself prominent members like 'Billy' Hughes, and even Spender himself, were rumoured to be implicated, though both issued public denials. There were other, lesser, members of the party—men like William McCall, Sir Charles Marr and William Hutchinson—whose enmity was open and long-standing, reflecting resentment at having been passed over when Menzies had chosen ministers, personal pique at Menzies' seeming arrogance, or disaffection because of Menzies' unpopularity with certain parts of the electorate.

The Prime Minister's initial reception momentarily belied the dark forebodings he felt on the eve of his arrival home. The *Sydney Morning Herald* struck a positive note in a welcoming editorial, headed 'Native Son's Return: Horoscope for Mr Menzies', which spoke of a 'flood tide' waiting for the returning Menzies. Fadden had done an excellent job in 'promoting mutual understanding among Australian political parties', and Menzies' own prestige abroad and commitment to new vigour at this desperate juncture of the war promised inspired leadership. And when, after resting in seclusion with his wife for thirty-six hours, Menzies made his first public appearance at the Sydney Town Hall on the evening of Monday 26 May he received a tumultuous welcome. The hall was packed and loudspeakers carried his words to the overflow crowd in the street outside. He had prepared well and the adrenalin flowed as he spoke on the subject that most deeply moved him. At the end the audience cheered wildly, rose to their feet and spontaneously sang 'For he's a jolly good fellow'. Next day the main newspapers of the country were unanimous in declaring the speech he made as one which 'for passionate eloquence and emotional fervour must surely have been the greatest of his career'.[11] The burden of the speech was a declaration of Menzies' pride in the Australians he had seen in the Middle East, and a moving account of the courage he had witnessed in Britain in the face of 'utter human anguish'. These things had a deep message for Australia:

> We must begin to change our lives; we must make up our minds that war
> of this magnitude against an enemy of this strength and power can only

10   Percy Spender, *Politics and a Man* (Sydney, 1972), p. 158.
11   *Argus*, 27 May 1941.

be won by completely organizing every bit of our energy for his defeat ...
every bomb I have heard fall, every life I have seen ruined, every
experience that I have seen people go through in Great Britain ... has left
me more convinced that the time has gone by for the old fights in our
country. There is one fight only that matters today and I call on the whole
of Australia to GO TO IT![12]

At the civic reception that followed, an elated Menzies met Spender. 'Well
Percy, where is this grave you wrote about?' Spender replied: 'It's been dug all
right Bob: it is only waiting for you to be pushed into it.'[13] A few days later
Menzies received a less happy reception when he formally reported to Parliament
on his trip and again complained querulously about the political dissension he
alleged he found in Australia. But he survived this, met the Advisory War
Council, and then went home to Melbourne to receive a hero's welcome from
crowd-lined streets and a packed Town Hall.

These were the apparently triumphant heights from which, over the next
few months, Menzies rapidly fell until, in September, Spender's prediction
proved all too correct. The work of the 'gravediggers' was only a part of what
happened, but it was an important part. They were pre-eminent among those
who sedulously spread the idea that Menzies did not command the authority
and popular loyalty necessary to lead the nation in this time of crisis. Though the
Government took drastic new steps to put the country on a total war footing,
there was widespread resistance and the idea gained ground that the Prime
Minister was a man more of eloquent words than of deeds. Part of the
importance of the Diary is that it disproves the thrust of this general allegation,
but whether the allegation was or was not true is, in retrospect, almost irrelevant:
the important facts were that many believed it, and that the necessity to maintain
wartime secrecy prevented the Government from publicising what its
achievements were in defence, munitions production and general mobilisation.
Menzies was also unfortunate in that his return to Australia coincided with the
end of the short and disastrous Greek and Cretan campaigns, and just as casualty
lists began to come through. Again, the requirements of wartime confidentiality
made it impossible for him to reveal his protests in the British War Cabinet, and
his opponents, both his own 'gravediggers' and prominent men in the
Opposition, managed to associate him politically with the mistakes of these ill-
starred operations. On this and other matters Menzies received a bad press.
Particularly vicious were Keith Murdoch's Melbourne *Herald* and Warwick
Fairfax's *Sydney Morning Herald*. The former was not impressed by Menzies'

12   *Sydney Morning Herald*, 27 May 1941.
13   Spender, *Politics and a Man*, p. 158.

successes in London and pursued what Menzies himself ironically called a policy of some subtlety, 'praising me and killing me in the same breath, the technique being that of the skilled slaughterman who calls attention to the beauties of the beast just as he strikes it down'. By contrast, he found the *Sydney Morning Herald*'s approach more direct: simply that of cutting him down 'blatantly and crudely'.[14] Two influences seem to have been of particular importance here. One was a bitter quarrel which Menzies had at this time with Fairfax over newsprint rationing, and which seems to have brought their friendship to an abrupt end.[15] The other was the animus often shown towards Menzies by the paper's Canberra correspondent, Ross Gollan, who had taken over his job after the 1940 election, and who in 1941 harped on the notion that Fadden's work during Menzies' absence in London marked him as the coming prime minister.

Particularly in the light of his experience in England, Menzies agreed with those, both friends and critics, who wanted to see the formation of a national, all-party government in Australia. On a number of occasions Menzies offered portfolios in such a government to the Labor Party, and in the end intimated that he would himself serve under another prime minister mutually agreed upon (even if he were a Labor leader) if a national government could be formed. But Labor's Executive had firmly ruled against such a coalition, and Curtin and the Parliamentary Caucus adhered rigidly to this policy. The leadership question came to a head in the last weeks of July when dissidents under William McCall demanded a joint UAP–Country Party meeting to reconsider it. Menzies called a UAP meeting and had his position confirmed, but it was an open secret that a joint party meeting would almost certainly have toppled him. At this juncture a marked deterioration in relations with Japan, which was evidently poised to invade Thailand, brought war in the Pacific perilously close and Menzies—pressed, among others, by Bruce in London and by his own Cabinet at home—decided he must go back to seek succour from the British War Cabinet. Churchill, with a canny eye on the troublesome Australian, had meantime made it clear that no Dominion Minister would be admitted to the British War Cabinet other than Prime Ministers currently in office. Given the tenuous nature of his hold on office, with his party in a minority in the House of Representatives, surviving only at the pleasure of two Independents, Menzies could not go to England without the understanding, which he had had on his previous trip, that Labor permitted it. But when he sought agreement to this, the

---

14   R.G. Menzies, personal account of events leading up to his resignation, dated 1 September 1941, Menzies Family Papers.

15   Gavin Souter, *Company of Heralds* (Melbourne, 1981) has in his chapter 6 a fascinating account of Menzies' relations with Fairfax and the *Sydney Morning Herald*, from which the points made here are drawn.

Parliamentary Labor Party refused, on the ground that at a time of acute crisis, the Prime Minister's place was in his own country. Menzies was trapped. He could not assume, if he went to England, that his Ministry, lacking his vote in the House, would be safe. Yet he would only be admitted to the British War Cabinet as long as he was Prime Minister of Australia.

In the face of this intractable situation Menzies announced his readiness to serve under Curtin if a national government could be formed. When the Labor Party turned down that offer Menzies, after a tense Cabinet meeting which revealed Ministers to be deeply divided over his leadership, and after anxious family consultations, decided to resign. He felt, as he wrote next day, that 'my political leadership clearly rested upon nothing better than quicksands', and he could not agree to the fierce urging of those Ministers who were faithful to him and wanted him to fight and take the issue to the people. He expected that, if there were an election, Labor would win it. And he believed that under Labor the distant war in Europe and the Middle East would not be prosecuted with full vigour. Better, he reasoned, for his coalition to choose a new leader who might bring its internal dissidents to heel and carry on with the vital work the Government already had in hand.

Menzies made it a condition of his resignation that his successor should be chosen by a joint meeting of the Parliamentary UAP and Country Party. To that meeting he formally tendered his resignation, and two of the UAP dissidents, Hutchinson and Marr, nominated Fadden of the Country Party as the new leader. There was no other nomination. At this point, according to Menzies' account, he simply 'issued statement to press, and went home'. His private secretary, Cecil Looker, later remembered that it was somewhat less matter of fact than that. He and Menzies, he said, left the party meeting just after midnight. With his arm around Looker's shoulders and tears in his eyes, Menzies blurted out words which Looker recollected as 'I have been done ... I'll lie down and bleed awhile'.[16] The statement for the press was honest and dignified. Labor had rejected the offer of an all-party Ministry, even without him as Prime Minister:

> It follows that the next task is to get the greatest possible stability and cohesion on the Government side of the House.
>
> A frank discussion with my colleagues in the Cabinet has shown that, while they have personal good will toward me, many of them feel that I am unpopular with large sections of the Press and the people; that this unpopularity handicaps the effectiveness of the Government by giving

16   Interview on ABC television, 19 February 1984, with Huw Evans. A similar story is recounted by Gavin Souter, *Acts of Parliament* (Melbourne, 1988), p. 340.

rise to misrepresentation and misunderstanding of its activities; and that there are divisions of opinion in the Government parties themselves which would or might not exist under another leader.

It is not for me to be the judge of these matters, except to this extent, that I do believe that my relinquishing of the leadership will offer real prospects of unity in the ranks of the Government parties. In these circumstances, and having regard to the grave emergencies of war, my own feelings must be set aside.[17]

Next day Menzies returned his commission and wrote gracefully to Curtin: 'Your political opposition has been honourable and your personal friendship a pearl of great price.' 'On my part,' Curtin replied, 'I thank you for the consideration and courtesy which never once failed in your dealings with me.'[18] Perhaps that caught the spirit of the moment, and helped the fallen Prime Minister to cope with the pain.

---

17   *Argus*, 29 August 1941.

18   Menzies to Curtin and Curtin to Menzies, 29 August 1941, Menzies Family Papers.

Appendix I

THE GREEK CAMPAIGN

On the fall of France in mid-1940, Italy entered the war on the side of Nazi Germany. In October Mussolini's troops invaded Greece, and the first Axis thrust into the Balkans began. But Italy suffered serious losses and by the end of the year it became clear that, if a disastrous defeat was not to follow, the Germans would have to come to Italy's aid. As far back as April 1939 the Chamberlain Government had given Greece a promise of support in the event of an Axis attack, and whether Britain would now help the Greeks became an issue. Only a little assistance in the air at first seemed possible: then Wavell's dramatic victories in North Africa raised the possibility that, if Suez could be considered safe, some British troops in the Middle East (of which one New Zealand and two Australian divisions were the most important) could be spared to assist Greece. Wavell himself had for some time been concerned lest a German drive on the north-eastern Greek frontier threaten the port of Salonika, access to which allowed British control of the eastern Mediterranean.[1]

The problem came to a head in February 1941, just as Menzies reached the Middle East. The Greeks had formally appealed for help, and behind the scenes Churchill was keen, both on sentimental and strategic grounds, for Britain to come to their aid. He had the somewhat bizarre idea that such an action might encourage Yugoslavia and Turkey, so far strictly neutral, into the war, to make with Greece and Britain a formidable Balkan anti-German alliance. On 12 February Anthony Eden, the Foreign Secretary, and General Sir John Dill, Chief of the Imperial General Staff, left London; sent by the British War Cabinet to discuss the Greek situation with Wavell and the Middle East service chiefs. Bad weather, in which their flying boat was almost lost, delayed them at Gibraltar, and they did not arrive in Cairo until 19 February. Wavell remarked that the emissaries had been a long time coming, and told them that he had already begun bringing troops together for dispatch to Greece. Indeed, on the day before Eden and Dill arrived, he had sent for Blamey and told him of 'plans he had made for the organization of a force designated "Lustreforce"' for operations in Greece.[2] These were evidently the basis of the agreement to which Wavell, Eden, Dill and the service chiefs quickly came, to recommend that Lustreforce be dispatched to

---

1   Field-Marshal Earl Wavell, 'The British Expedition to Greece, 1941', *The Army Quarterly*, vol. LIX, no. 2, January 1950, pp. 178–9.

2   Blamey to Minister for the Army, 12 March 1941, AA A5954/1/528/1.

Greece. It was this recommendation, subsequently examined and approved by the Imperial General Staff, which was put to the War Cabinet on 24 February, at the first meeting Menzies attended. Meantime Eden and Dill had gone on to Greece, to discuss plans with Greek politicians and the commander there, General Papagos.

Menzies left Cairo on 14 February, five days before Eden and Dill arrived, and therefore well before the firm decision was taken to recommend the Greek expedition. How far Wavell had formed precise plans before Menzies left, and whether he had talked them over with Menzies, remains obscure. One historian, who is convinced that he had and did, quotes a signal which Wavell sent to the Chiefs of Staff in London on 12 February saying that a strengthened force could be sent to Greece 'if the Australian Government will give me certain latitude as regards the use of their troops. I have already spoken to Menzies about this, and he was very ready to agree to what I suggest. I shall approach him again before he leaves.'[3] Blamey himself, in reporting some weeks after the event Wavell's first mention to him of Lustreforce, added: 'I informed him that in my view the matter would require to be referred to Australia, and he stated that he had discussed the possibility of such an operation with the Prime Minister of Australia.'[4] Blamey maintained that though he saw much of Menzies during the latter's visit, the Prime Minister never mentioned the impending expedition, a strange omission, given that Blamey was the commander of the AIF forces that were to be used.

Menzies' Diary suggests one answer to this puzzle. It is possible that he did not speak to Blamey about the impending expedition simply because he knew of no definite plans. Though he records meeting Wavell on various occasions, he makes no mention of Greece until the evening before his departure. That was the day on which Wavell had told the Chiefs of Staff that 'I shall approach him again'. Menzies simply records on 13 February: 'Back at 8 pm to an interview with Wavell, who is clearly contemplating the possibility of a Salonika expedition.' To contemplate the possibility (and, as Blamey reported Wavell's words to him, to 'discuss the possibility') is not to put forward clear plans or ask for a commitment. Perhaps Wavell was dissembling or perhaps he still, in the next five days, had yet to work out the distinct plans he would present to Eden and Dill. The probability is that what discussion he had with Menzies was general and of a kind likely to elicit vague approval involving no precise commitment. This possibility is underlined by the emotion that comes through in the Diary when Churchill, at Chequers on the eve of Menzies' first

---

3   Norman D. Carlyon, *I Remember Blamey* (Melbourne, 1980), p. 27.
4   Blamey to Minister for the Army, 12 March 1941, AA A5954/1/528/1.

War Cabinet appearance, reveals the plans for the expedition, and by the anxious talks Menzies had with Bruce and Shedden on the eve of that fateful Cabinet meeting on 24 February. If Menzies already knew about the expedition it seems strange that it should now be the cause of such soul-searching. It was of course in Wavell's interest to blow up the importance of any chance remarks Menzies had made when they talked. It is not without significance that Menzies, like a number of others, saw something withdrawn, perhaps sinister, in Wavell's mien. The General's deviousness is suggested by a message he sent to Churchill on 30 March 1941, when Lustreforce was under way and both Menzies and Blamey had registered their unhappiness with his methods:

> I am sorry if Blamey thinks I have not kept him sufficiently in picture, I thought I had been particularly careful to give him as much consideration as possible. It is true I did not consult him previous to our agreement with Greece. I do not think it would have been possible or politic to do so, but I had previously outlined to him possibility of our intervening in Greece and took him into my confidence immediately afterwards. Please assure Menzies I do my best and while Blamey was in Palestine sent him periodically my appreciation of Middle East situation and outline of my intentions.[5]

Menzies' Diary, as well as War Cabinet Minutes, make it clear that at the meeting of 24 February he insisted that the Australian Cabinet must agree to the AIF deployment in the operation and asked more questions, many of them aggressive, than any others present about the guarantees of succour for the soldiers should things go wrong. Doubtful Cabinet agreement from Australia was forthcoming.[6] But then, a little over a week later, Eden and Dill, still in Athens, sent word of unexpected planning difficulties with the Greek command. General Papagos, with whom, it was now revealed, Dill had without authorisation made an agreement, was proving 'unaccommodating and defeatist'. He had failed to honour promises to consolidate Greek forces on an agreed defensive line, and though two days of anxious talks had brought some improvement in Greek morale, 'the hard fact remains that our forces, including Dominion contingents, will be engaged in an operation more hazardous than it seemed a week ago'.[7]

---

5   Private and Confidential, Wavell to Churchill, 30 March 1941, Churchill Archives Centre, Cambridge, CHAR 20/37. We are indebted to the Master and Fellows of Churchill College for permission to quote from this document.

6   Menzies to Fadden, 25 February 1941, and Fadden to Menzies, 26 February 1941, *DAFP*, vol. IV, pp. 452–5.

7   Eden and Chief of Imperial General Staff to Churchill, 5 March 1940, PRO CAB 65/22/17–18.

Churchill's first reaction to this news was one of alarm and momentary clear-headedness. 'We must be careful not to urge Greece against her better judgement into a hopeless resistance alone when we have only handfuls of troops which can reach scene in time,' he wired Eden. Besides, Australian and New Zealand troops would be primarily involved, and their Governments' agreement to their use in changed circumstances might be doubtful. And after all, 'loss of Greece and Balkans by no means a major catastrophe for us provided Turkey remains honest neutral'.[8] Eden, however, was greatly annoyed by such an idea. 'I need not emphasise to you,' he telegraphed back, 'the effect of our now withdrawing from the agreement actually signed between Chief of the Imperial General Staff and Greek Commander-in-Chief ... This seems to me quite unthinkable. We shall be pilloried by the Greeks and the world in general as going back on our word.'[9]

When these messages were reported to the War Cabinet, Menzies launched a bitter protest at the way the whole affair was being handled. The Australian Government, he said, had accepted the plan for a Greek expedition with reluctance; now new difficulties were being revealed. And Eden's admission that a military agreement between Dill and Papagos had been signed was, to say the least, embarrassing. Was he, Menzies, to tell his colleagues that the Australians and New Zealanders, who would provide three-fifths of the forces to be used, were committed by an agreement, signed in Athens, which had not even been referred home to Britain, let alone the subject of proper consultation with the Dominions themselves?[10] Churchill at first took the point, cabling military headquarters in Cairo:

> We must be able to tell the Australian and New Zealand Governments that the campaign was undertaken, not because of any commitment entered into by a British Cabinet Minister in Athens, but because the Chief of the Imperial General Staff and the Commander-in-Chief in the Middle East were convinced that there was a reasonable fighting chance. So far, few facts or reasons have been supplied which could be represented as justifying the operation on any grounds but *noblesse oblige*. A precise military appreciation is indispensable.[11]

When this telegram was reported to the War Cabinet, Menzies declared that it 'expressed his own views with precision', but if he hoped there would be a delay at least until the appreciation arrived, he was mistaken. Suddenly Churchill,

---

8   Churchill to Eden, 5 March 1941, PRO CAB 65/18/13.

9   War Cabinet Minutes, Eden to Churchill, 6 March 1941, PRO CAB 65/22/23ff.

10   Ibid. And see Menzies 1941 Diary, 5 and 6 March.

11   War Cabinet Minutes, 7 March 1941, PRO CAB 65/18/19.

no doubt stung by Eden's indignant cable, demanded immediate action. 'A considered military appreciation,' he said, was 'on the way here from Cairo [to] supply the detailed arguments; but we know the conclusions already.' In the circumstances it was 'our duty to go forward, making the necessary communications to the Dominions whose forces were to take part in the campaign'. The War Cabinet endorsed Churchill's view and asked Menzies to obtain the agreement of his Government. At the same time a message from Dill was tabled, saying that Wavell had explained the situation to Blamey and Major-General Bernard Freyberg (the New Zealand commander), and both had 'expressed their willingness to undertake operations under new conditions'.[12] In the circumstances Menzies could only cable his Acting Prime Minister, Arthur Fadden, sending copies of recent telegrams on the Greek issue, saying that Eden, Dill and Wavell thought there was a good prospect of success and that Wavell had given assurances that troops could now be drawn off without endangering his position on the Benghazi front.[13] In reply Fadden expressed resentment at Eden and Dill having without consultation entered into an agreement which affected Australian troops, and registered the Australian Cabinet's fear that if there should be a defeat and evacuation in Greece that could have a severe effect on Japan's attitude to Australia. But still, Cabinet knew that the troops if committed to battle would 'worthily uphold the glorious traditions of the A.I.F.'[14] In fact the military appreciation which Churchill asked for, and whose expected arrival he used to justify the move to embark on the campaign, appears never to have been made.[15] And three days *before* Menzies sent Fadden his recommendation that the Australian Government agree to the expedition the first echelons of the AIF were ordered to embark for Greece.[16]

---

12   Ibid. Blamey later claimed that he had expressed no view on this matter. 'On 6th March I was again called in and saw the Chief of the Imperial General Staff (General Sir John Dill) with the Commander-in-Chief. I was informed that following on a visit of the Commander-in-Chief to Greece there was some doubt as to the plans developing. Although both on this and on the previous visits my views were not asked for and I felt I was receiving instructions, I made enquiries as to what other formations would be available and when.' Blamey to Minister for the Army, 12 March 1941, AA A5954/1/528/1.

13   Menzies to Fadden, 8 March 1941, *DAFP*, vol. IV, pp. 484–6.

14   Fadden to Menzies, 10 March 1941, *DAFP*, vol. IV, p. 487.

15   No such document exists in the British War Cabinet papers. Shedden, in an unpublished account of the background to the Greek campaign, quotes Lord Ismay's *Memoirs* to the effect that Wavell and Eden simply ignored Churchill's request, 'at a critical stage, to submit "a precise military appreciation" to confirm opinions expressed by [them], such as "we believe there is a fair chance of halting a German advance, and preventing Greece from being overrun".' AA A5954/1/766/19.

16   Gavin Long, *Greece, Crete and Syria* (Sydney, 1986), p. 23 notes the embarkation on 5 March 1941.

Early in April disaster threatened simultaneously in the Middle East and Greece. The German General Erwin Rommel had arrived in Tripoli in February to begin building up an armoured force, the Africa Corps, to help the Italians. He worked more speedily and his seaward supply lines were less interrupted by the British navy than Wavell had anticipated, and on 31 March an offensive westward began. Wavell had made a serious miscalculation: by now the AIF 6th Division and the New Zealanders were in Greece. The Australian 7th Division was hastily retained to help in the defence of Egypt, but the forces at Wavell's disposal were no match for the speed and weight of Rommel's armour. Soon most were in retreat, in a short time losing all the ground they had won only a few months earlier. The one British stand was made at the port of Tobruk, then garrisoned by the Australian 9th Division, one brigade of the 7th and some British units. By 11 April the city was completely invested by land and the heroic resistance had begun. As Menzies' Diary notes on 7 and 11 April testify, he was horrified at the news of Rommel's victories. In the War Cabinet he berated the way 'our generals consistently underestimate Germany's capacity'. He aggressively quizzed the First Sea Lord about the navy's failure to cut off what he sardonically called the Germans' 'regular ferry service' of supplies to Tripoli, and was dismayed to learn that German dive-bombers based on Sicily and Tripoli and outside the range of British fighters (from Malta) made naval attack on Axis convoys extremely hazardous. Largely at his insistence the Admiralty was instructed that 'great risks must be taken' to disrupt the German supply system.[17]

German forces moved into Yugoslavia on 6 April. They were soon through to the Greek border, and with their heavy armour and almost complete mastery of the air swept upon the defending forces with relentless power. Though the invaders suffered heavy casualties, resistance quickly crumbled and on 16 April Wavell informed Dill that a stand would be made at Thermopylae to cover embarking troops and that all ships still coming to Greece with troops must turn back.[18] Australian units established the Thermopylae Line on 19 April, but Blamey warned that, lacking air cover, they would not be able to hold out long. Churchill ordered it 'to be made plain to the Commander-in-Chief that the main thing was to get the men away, and that we should not worry about saving vehicles'.[19] In the War Cabinet Menzies appealed desperately for more air cover to be provided for the retreating troops, but Churchill insisted that Libya must have priority over the limited air resources available.[20] The main evacuation

---

17   War Cabinet Minutes, 11 April 1941, PRO CAB 65/18/77 and CAB 65/22.

18   War Cabinet Minutes, 16 April 1941, PRO CAB 65/22/124.

19   War Cabinet Minutes, 21 April 1941, PRO CAB 65/18/87.

20   War Cabinet Minutes, 24 April 1941, PRO CAB 65/22/135.

took place over several nights from 25 April. Vehicles and heavy weapons were lost, but in other respects the evacuation was more successful than many hoped. More than 50 000 men got away—as Alexander Cadogan, head of the Foreign Office, noted dryly in his diary, this was the one thing 'we're really good at!'[21]— though 14 000, including 2000 Australians, were left behind.[22] Some of the remnants were almost immediately involved in a short and bloody attempt to defend Crete against German paratroops.

The full implications of the two disasters, which had lost Britain all the gains made in the Middle East in the previous three months, severely damaged her prestige and ruined two of Wavell's finest fighting divisions (the Australian 6th and the New Zealand 2nd), had still to be understood. But the dark days of anxiety, as events on the ground unfolded, provoked in Menzies the bitter feelings against Churchill and the British generals that colour the last part of his Diary. These feelings were exacerbated as news came through from Australia of charges that, though on the spot in London, it appeared that he had done little to interfere or protest as one mistake followed another. That he could never reveal publicly how much he had in the War Cabinet worried and protested no doubt exacerbated his chagrin. As he left for home, Menzies was convinced that more disaster lay ahead unless a curb was put on Churchill, and that this could be done only if a strong Dominion man were added to the War Cabinet to act—as he and Lloyd George agreed—as a 'prop' for the Prime Minister.

---

21   Dilks, *Diaries of Sir Alexander Cadogan*, p. 374.

22   Jeffrey Grey, *A Military History of Australia* (Cambridge, 1990), p. 158.

Appendix II

THE TRIP TO IRELAND

When Menzies left Australia in January 1941 he had given little thought to Ireland: Singapore, Australia's position in the Pacific and the feats of Australian arms in the Middle East were the concerns uppermost in his mind. But from the moment of his arrival in England he repeatedly encountered, and was soon himself deeply concerned about, the Irish question. It was the main topic of conversation at his first London luncheon, Churchill fulminated about it almost every time Menzies visited Chequers, it came under repeated discussion as he sat in the British War Cabinet.

In the grim circumstances of 1941, it was difficult for the English not to be embittered by Prime Minister Eamon de Valera's steely determination to keep the Republic of Eire out of the war. Her neutrality was causing a number of unhappy results, the most damaging of which was denial of access to the 'Treaty Ports'. These were five facilities—harbours at Berehaven, Cobh and Lough Swilly, and fuel storages at Haulbowline and Rathmullan—originally retained under British control in the Treaty of 1921 which had given independence to Eire. To acquire the Treaty Ports at once became a prime aim of Irish nationalists, and in 1938 de Valera managed successfully to negotiate with the Chamberlain Government for their surrender. Predictably, Churchill was appalled. When the decision was announced in the House of Commons, he exploded:

> I say that the ports may be denied to us in the hour of need and we may be hampered in the gravest manner in protecting the British population from privation and even starvation. Who would wish to put his head in such a noose? Is there any other country in the modern world where such a step would even have been contemplated?[1]

But, as the historian R.F. Foster has recently shown, the Ports

> were handed over with curiously little deliberation on the British side; in some ways, their upkeep was seen as a liability, and there was a general expectation (not to be fulfilled) that in time of war they might be made available again. The Chiefs of Staff acquiesced in this gesture of

---

[1]   House of Commons, *Parliamentary Debates*, 1938, vol. 335, col. 1103.

Chamberlainite appeasement as regrettable but inevitable; the infuriated Churchill was in a small minority.[2]

When the war broke out and Ireland refused use of the Ports, Churchill in particular repeatedly made inflammatory statements and, as Menzies' Diary shows, a real fear developed after Churchill became Prime Minister that the British might try to regain the Ports by force. In fact, though Menzies did not know it, Churchill had ordered in 1940 the preparation of a plan (code-named 'Alcohol') to occupy the Ports 'in the event of a worsening of the naval situation'.[3] When Menzies arrived in London the naval situation had indeed worsened. Left fighting alone by the fall of France, enduring German bombing and hourly expecting a German invasion, Britain seemed also in danger of being choked to death by catastrophic shipping losses on her western lifeline. Between July and October 1940, 245 vessels were sunk in the Atlantic, and in November, the worst month of the year, 73 went to the bottom. In February 1941, the month in which Menzies reached London, the greatest single monthly loss since the beginning of the war was recorded: 79 ships.[4] As he sat in the War Cabinet, Menzies became well aware of what was happening. 'Another convoy beaten up', he records on 27 February. 'The shipping strain is enormous, and represents our only real chance of defeat.' We now know that the Atlantic losses of this period resulted partly from a disastrous lapse in security which enabled German intelligence to break British naval codes and pinpoint for U-boat packs the exact location of convoys.[5] It was nevertheless also true that bases like Berehaven would have given Britain a wider range for anti-submarine operations in the Atlantic and would have provided convoys with better protection. By 1941 the Luftwaffe had perfected tactics which added new ravages to those of the U-boats. Focke-Wulf Condor bombers regularly preyed on the mainstream of traffic up the Mayo coast to Malin Head. The big four-engined aircraft flew from French airfields at Brest over to the west coast of Ireland, to cross back, when their tanks were low on fuel, to bases at Stavanger in German-occupied Norway. At Berehaven, where British fighters and anti-aircraft batteries might have been stationed, local people watched these planes fly past, undisturbed, every morning *en route* for the Atlantic convoy lines. As the historian Robert Fisk has written, in the emotional climate of that time 'the Irish Government could not escape the

---

2   R.F. Foster, *Modern Ireland, 1600–1972* (London, 1988), p. 554.

3   Martin Gilbert, *Winston S. Churchill, vol. VI: Finest Hour 1939–1941* (London, 1983), p. 574.

4   Robert Fisk, *In Time of War* (Philadelphia, 1983), pp. 247 and 260.

5   Ibid., p. 250.

accusation ... that dead British seamen were being washed up on Eire's shores because of her policy of neutrality'.[6]

This was the background against which, at Chequers on 9 March, Menzies met Colonel William Donovan, who was then a kind of roving ambassador for President Roosevelt, and (as the record of the event in his Diary shows) a man with whom Menzies at once clicked. He could not of course know that Donovan had close connections with the British Secret Service and that in recent visits to the Balkans and the Middle East had been deeply involved in the confidential on-the-spot discussions which led to the fatal recommendation that British troops intervene in Greece. Donovan had just been in Ireland and Menzies was impressed by his views on de Valera's possible tractability. Donovan thought that if only de Valera and Churchill could be persuaded to meet, a fruitful understanding might yet be reached.[7] This conversation may very well have been the trigger for a rather daring idea that evidently took shape in Menzies' mind over the next few weeks. Could he, as a complete outsider, influential but untainted by any previous association with Ireland, step in and do something to break the impasse? While he pondered this, the Irish situation became more tense. By late March British restrictions on trade and shipping to Ireland had reduced the petrol allowance to private motorists by 75 per cent, brought tea rationing and the end of wheat imports needed for the supply of white bread, and had cut off external supplies of oil, fat and sugar. These matters were discussed in detail on 24 March in the War Cabinet, whose minutes record agreement on the importance 'from the political point of view that the pressure on Eire should be fully maintained'. Menzies announced at the same meeting that he was arranging to meet de Valera, 'and he thought it might be of assistance if this talk was to be followed by some public statement of his views on the Eire position'.[8] There is no contemporary evidence of Churchill's reaction to this decision. But in memoirs written some years later Menzies recalled that Churchill had said to him: 'Never with my approval will you visit that wicked man.'[9]

Menzies' Diary vividly records what were for him the salient experiences of the short time between his flight to Northern Ireland on 3 April and his homecoming to Heston two packed days later.[10] Local newspapers, which were puzzled by his mission and took a good deal of notice of him, flesh out his account of the visit. It was certainly the case that at the Ulster Reform Club his

---

6   Ibid., pp. 252 and 259–60.

7   Menzies 1941 Diary, 9 March.

8   War Cabinet Minutes, 24 March 1941, PRO CAB 65/18/45.

9   Menzies, *Afternoon Light*, p. 37.

10   Menzies 1941 Diary, 3–5 April.

speech was 'acclaimed in extravagant terms': Andrews, the Prime Minister, described it as a very great speech: 'one of the greatest ever heard in the Club.' Menzies had begun with jocular remarks hardly tactful for a man about to go to Dublin. He felt quite at home in the Ulster Club, he said, for the best Northern Irelanders were like the best Australians: 'improved Scotsmen.' But his main theme was clearly directed at the Eire he would visit the next day. It was that of loyalty to the Commonwealth's one King: 'When that ... King makes war and makes it, as on the present occasion, most justly, then I have never felt inclined as a representative of my own country to sit down and engage in vague speculation as to whether or not I should declare war.'[11] That evening he held a relaxed press conference. 'Installing himself in a chair at the head of the tables in the Senate Room of Queen's,' reported the *Belfast Telegraph*, 'he got a briar pipe going well and then invited questions from all and sundry.' Menzies parried questions about the Treaty Ports, denied that he brought messages to de Valera from Churchill and said that his only aim was to see Ireland for himself and give de Valera the greetings of the Australian people.[12]

Next day Menzies travelled by train to Dublin, where he was met at the Amiens Street station by Joseph Walshe, Secretary to the Irish Department of External Affairs, and given a police guard of honour. The Dublin *Evening Mail* reported 'some handclapping from the small crowd which had gathered as the tall, immaculately clad figure of the Australian Prime Minister stepped from the carriage', and it and the Dublin *Evening Herald* carried front-page pictures of Menzies, with Walshe at his side and Homburg hat in his hand, inspecting the policemen drawn stiffly up in line on the platform.[13] As recorded in the Diary, Menzies then had his long and cathartic interview with de Valera, his trip around Dublin, and the press conference on the eve of his departure. Journalists in Dublin got as little satisfaction out of Menzies as had their brethren in Belfast. Again he refused to be drawn on the Treaty Ports or to say what he and de Valera had talked about. He had no sympathy for Irish complaints about British restrictions on trade and supplies: 'Everybody here seems to live a full life.'[14] Back in London by 6 April, Menzies got at once to work on a careful report for the War Cabinet of his experiences and recommendations. It was finished and discussed in Cabinet four days later.

Menzies' report is a remarkable document, the work of a man not expert in the intricacies of Irish politics and history but, as acute lawyer and politician,

---

11   *Belfast Telegraph*, 3 April 1941.
12   Ibid., 4 April 1941; also *Irish Times* for the same date.
13   4 April 1941.
14   Dublin *Saturday Herald*, 5 April 1941; *Irish Times*, 7 April 1941.

skilled in the arts of observation, digestion and empathy.[15] His natural prejudices were challenged at the very outset of his trip:

> There is a very strong and indeed bitter feeling in Ulster about Eire. Though the whole of my own instinctive bias is in favour of Ulster, I was occasionally a little disturbed to find myself wondering whether the Ulster attitude is entirely a reasoned one. Just as there are some Protestants whose Protestantism is an expression of hostility rather than of faith, so there are undoubtedly Ulstermen whose loyalty to Great Britain seems chiefly founded upon a dislike of the South.

This caveat having been recorded, Menzies goes on to comment on the industrial, employment and recruiting problems of Northern Ireland. It is a sympathetic, if somewhat lifeless account. But when he turns to Eire, this 'distressful country', as he calls it, the discussion takes on a new animation. A real live person appears on centre stage: de Valera.

> He interested me very much. He is at first sight a somewhat saturnine figure, particularly when he sallies abroad in a long dark frieze overcoat and a broad brimmed black hat. Personal contact with him, however, indicates that he is ... I think sincere, and with a mind in which acute intelligence is found to contain many blind spots occasioned by prejudice, bitter personal experience, and a marked slavery to past history ... He has a large and fanatical following in Dublin. He is the 'chief'. The very clerks in the offices stand promptly to attention as he strides past. His Ministers speak with freedom in his absence, but are restrained and obedient in his presence. Some of these Ministers are possessed of more flexible minds than his, and I found them merry fellows, but in the last resort I am quite sure that his view will prevail. On the whole, with all my prejudices, I liked him and occasionally succeeded in invoking from him a sort of wintry humour, which was not without charm.

In attempting to summarise de Valera's views Menzies declares his conviction that the Irish leader sees the British cause in the war as a just one, but equally believes that Churchill's Government is hostile and unwilling to grasp Ireland's anxieties. He notes de Valera's anger at alleged injustices to Catholics in

---

15   Copy no. 12 of this memorandum is in the Menzies Papers, National Library of Australia MS 4936/1/5/36. It was also published in *DAFP*, vol. IV, pp. 549–54 after the Australian thirty-year embargo had expired. The quotations in what follows are from these sources. A fifty-year embargo was originally placed on the document in Britain and it was still unavailable at the Public Record Office in 1986 but was presumably released in 1991.

Northern Ireland, but thinks this rather 'shadowy', and avers that when brought face to face with his most fundamental grievance, de Valera admits that it is quite unrealistic to imagine that Britain will ever be a party to an enforced absorption of Ulster into Eire. He observes how, when asked to explain what he means by his assertion of the 'passionate desire in the Irish heart to be neutral in the war', de Valera 'slipped easily and skilfully into a discussion of past history' but 'with some regularity' came back

> to another reason which struck me as much more comprehensible and much more capable of being dealt with. That reason was that 'Ireland is defenceless', that 'Dublin has ... practically no air force', and that 'the army is without modern equipment'. In other words, I am quite sure that De Valera's neutrality policy is founded not only upon a traditional distrust of Great Britain, but also and perhaps principally upon fear of German attack, particularly from the air.
> ... I was left, after many repetitions, with a very definite feeling that, as this fear of attack is the principal obsession, the possibility of removing it by some material assistance on the munitions and aircraft side should be promptly explored.

The encounter clearly had its bizarre side. The wily de Valera gave Menzies an impression of almost childlike innocence.

> He stands in front of the map and cannot understand why naval bases in Ireland should be of the slightest importance to Great Britain. I found it necessary to explain to him the importance of air bases as a platform for fighting aircraft. He did not appear to have appreciated the immense significance of even a hundred miles in the zone of operations of fighters. I think he would understand these things much better if he had some of his own.

Other arguments were adduced to support the theme of de Valera's naiveté, and it is evident that, despite his 'improved' Scottishness, Menzies was not immune to Irish blarney. That, and his tendency to assume that reason could overcome history, led him into a set of final conclusions which he must have sensed, even as he wrote them, would be scarcely acceptable to Churchill. Still, he did not pull his punches:

> The paragraphs I have written above contain, as I realise, much exasperating information ... [de Valera] has in my opinion some fine qualities. His fixed ideas, like those of his people, cannot be removed by

aloofness or by force. They can be removed only by a genuine attempt to get at their foundations by enquiry and, wherever possible, by understanding. To the outsider, like myself, and particularly to one who travelled seventeen thousand miles to confer with his colleagues of the British Government, it is fantastic to be told that De Valera and Andrews have never met, and that I have had more conversation with De Valera than any British Minister has had since the war began. I therefore suggest very strongly that the whole question of the defence of Eire should be looked at, that the Secretary of State for the Dominions should pay an early visit to Belfast and Dublin, and that if he receives the slightest encouragement he should invite De Valera and a couple of his colleagues to come to London for discussions with the Prime Minister and other members of the British Cabinet. I know that such a meeting would be welcomed by some members of the Irish Cabinet who are beginning to realise that neutrality has its defeats no less renowned than war; and I would be by no means pessimistic about the outcome.

This paper came before Cabinet on 10 April: Menzies' Diary records its reception. The central feature is Churchill's reaction: 'Winston describes my paper as "very readable"—a most damning comment.' The War Cabinet Minutes note that Menzies' paper 'met with a considerable measure of support', but that Cabinet nevertheless concluded that it was unlikely that de Valera could be persuaded to come to London, and that if he did no new results would be likely to follow. 'He already knew that if Eire was prepared to abandon its neutrality (a) we were ready to share our air defences with them; and (b) we would be ready to set up a Defence Council for All-Ireland, in the hope that a united Ireland might spring therefrom. There was nothing more we could tell them.'[16] This, of course, was in reality the voice of Churchill, whose apparent domination of Cabinet was at the base of Menzies' increasing alienation.

On Ireland Menzies could do no more: his spontaneously and carefully constructed report was dead. An embargo on its publication, as a Cabinet document, meant that it could not be disseminated or published. All that was left was to complain to the family. To his wife Menzies wrote ironically:

> I had a short but interesting visit to Ireland, about which I cannot write at length, but which I am quite sure you will enjoy hearing about on my return. On the whole I rather like De Valera (though you must tell this to Mother and Father with great discretion), even though I, of course, disagreed with almost everything he said.

---

16   War Cabinet Minutes, 10 April 1941, PRO CAB 65/18.

Personally, I think the Irish problem is soluble, and I have made an elaborate report on it to Cabinet here. But the greatest difficulty is the prevailing lunacy. They are mad in Dublin, madder still in Belfast, and on this question perhaps maddest of all at Downing Street. Blind prejudice, based on historical events, is the most intractable and almost the most dangerous thing in the world.[17]

Though an exasperated judgement it was perhaps instinctively close to the mark.

---

[17]   Menzies to Pat Menzies, 23 April 1941, Menzies Family Papers.

Appendix III

APPRAISING CHURCHILL

A recurrent theme throughout the Diary is Menzies' concern, sometimes shading into indignation, at Churchill's dictatorial handling of his War Cabinet and the British service chiefs, and the seeming unwillingness of Ministers, most of whom are depicted as 'yes-men', to stand up to Churchill or even to discuss matters of moment at any length. Not that, given the curious love-hate relationship he developed with the great man, Menzies was always consistent about this. Admiration at Churchill's genius often breaks through: 'it is superb to hear him cross examining and directing the experts. He is a marvellous master of all sorts of war-like detail, but contrary to impression, does not dictate to the experts. But he insists on <u>action</u>.'[1] However, Menzies' picture of Churchill as dictator, and erratic dictator at that, deepens in the last weeks of his stay in England. He has by this time suffered a wounding rebuff on Ireland, and is tortured with anxiety about the military situation in North Africa and Greece. He is determined that more considered reasoning than 'unilateral rhetoric' must decide the fate of Australian soldiers there.[2]

This view of Churchill was strengthened by some of the company Menzies kept during his last days in London. It included for example, Lord Hankey, 'man of a thousand secrets', who had wielded great influence between the wars as Secretary to the British Cabinet and also to the Committee of Imperial Defence, which until Churchill's accession to the prime ministership had made and administered policy on the Empire's defence. Before the war began in 1939 Churchill's predecessor, Neville Chamberlain, brought Hankey into the Cabinet as a full member. Churchill kept him on but associated him with discredited pre-war defence policies and allowed him no influence. Menzies had first met Hankey when the latter visited Melbourne in 1934, and their friendship grew during the former's visits to England in 1935, 1936 and 1938. At the time, in May 1941, of Menzies' imminent departure for Australia, Hankey attended a farewell lunch and shortly after, when walking away down Park Lane with his wife:

> We heard someone running, and low [sic] and behold, it was Menzies himself. He burst out at once about Churchill and his dictatorship and his War Cabinet of 'Yes-men'. 'There is only one thing to be done,' he said,

---

1   Menzies 1941 Diary, 9 March.
2   Ibid., 14 April.

'and that is to summon an Imperial War Cabinet and keep one of them behind, like Smuts in the last war, not as a guest but as a full member.' He was very much moved.[3]

Hankey could only agree: he considered Churchill's handling of strategy 'by a series of improvisations' extremely dangerous. 'I am puzzled what to do,' he told his diary. 'All my friends who were in the Chamberlain Government have been scattered.' One, however, Lord Simon, was still in the House of Lords. When Simon heard of Menzies' outburst he told Hankey that 'the best plan is to get Menzies to "bell the cat" before he leaves: he has become a great Imperial figure, has attended the War Cabinet ... for some weeks, has a big stake in the war and is entitled to speak his mind.' Hankey thereupon telephoned Menzies and begged that when farewelling Churchill he urge him 'to drop his dictatorial methods and to use his military and political advisers properly'.[4] Menzies' Diary is brief and enigmatic about the outcome: 'Confusion and hurry ... Long talk with Winston regarding the help he needs in Cabinet.'[5] But Shedden, who came to say goodbye to Hankey next day, said that Menzies 'got no change out of Churchill': his answer simply was 'you see the people by whom I am surrounded. They have no ideas, so the only thing to be done is to formulate my own ideas.' Hankey blew up. Of course that was the case: Churchill had got rid of anyone who had an independent mind because he was 'intolerant of other people's ideas and wants to be Dictator'.[6]

A few days before this Menzies had lunched with another man of the past who disapproved of Churchill: the seventy-eight-year-old Lloyd George. The two agreed to a long list of Churchill's failings, of which his tyrannical ways were the most prominent. These failings, they decided, pointed to an 'acute' need in Cabinet for 'a couple of good men to prop' the Prime Minister up.[7]

How accurate were these views of Churchill, particularly at this early and dispiriting stage of the war? In this matter it is important that the liveliness and passion of Menzies' Diary should not mislead the reader into thinking that what he observed was all that there was to see. Certainly, Churchill's forcefulness in policy-making, his independence, and his tendency to surrender to whim and romanticism are not to be denied. Nor is Menzies' observation of his vulnerability to 'the glittering phrase'.[8] That he nevertheless had extraordinary

---

3   Hankey Diary, 1 May 1941, Churchill Archives Centre, Cambridge.
4   Ibid., 2 May 1941.
5   Menzies 1941 Diary, 1–2 May.
6   Hankey Diary, 5 May 1941, Churchill Archives Centre, Cambridge.
7   Menzies 1941 Diary, 26 April.
8   Ibid., 2 March.

gifts for processing, memorising and creatively utilising information was agreed by most observers—including Menzies—to be the secret of much of his self-confidence and personal success. But there was also an organisational structure behind much of what appeared to be Churchill's 'dictatorship', and Menzies glimpsed this only occasionally and then without fully appreciating its significance.

The truth should have been evident to him from a very early stage of his visit when Anthony Eden, whom he knew from previous trips to England, rejoined the War Cabinet. As Foreign Secretary, Eden had been on a mission to Greece when Menzies arrived in London. On his first day back in Cabinet Eden found himself sitting beside Menzies, who passed him a note:

> 'This is the strangest Cabinet I ever sat in. Since you have been away I have only heard one voice. Do none of them ever speak up?' I explained to him afterwards how the technique worked. The War Cabinet did not wish to be immersed in the details of military operations. Whatever the Prime Minister had to say on these topics, which sometimes filled the greater part of our discussions, was not usually commented upon then, because it was the Defence Committee which handled those affairs.[9]

Under Churchill the Defence Committee became what he later called 'staff conferences': meetings between Churchill, the Chiefs of Staff and the one or two Ministers most directly concerned with whatever was the issue in hand. The Chiefs of Staff formed the pivot of the whole decision-making system. They were directly responsible to Churchill as Minister of Defence, a completely new post which he created for himself as soon as he became Prime Minister. The Chiefs of Staff met daily, on rare occasions summoned and chaired by Churchill himself. His usual contact with them was through Major-General Sir Hastings Ismay, who was head of the Office of the Minister of Defence and therefore in effect Churchill's personal staff officer. Ismay reported every day to Churchill on the deliberations of the Chiefs of Staff, and submitted reports and plans to Churchill for approval: 'Again and again, Churchill deferred to their collective advice, even when he disagreed with it, at times under formal protest. But he did not overrule them. Sometimes, indeed, it was they who turned to him.'[10]

Ismay's deputy, Colonel Leslie Hollis, recorded that 'the days of mere "co-ordination" were out for good and all. We were now going to get direction, leadership, action—with a snap in it!' As Churchill put it, the old system under the Committee of Imperial Defence seemed to represent 'the maximum of study and the minimum of action'. It was all very well, Hollis added, 'to say that

---

9   Anthony Eden, *Full Circle* (London, 1960), p. 447.

10   Gilbert, *Winston S. Churchill*, p. 325.

everything had been thought of. The crux of the matter was—had anything been done?'[11] It was no wonder, with this spirit animating it, that the new order was so uncongenial to Hankey!

The situation which Eden explained to Menzies was the product as much of these organisational arrangements as of any tyranny Churchill exercised over the War Cabinet. Menzies did briefly glimpse this once, at a Cabinet meeting on 4 March 1941. On this occasion, he records, Churchill made 'a short but impressive statement on war position ... Very simple but effective. Discussion very brief. Get through 3 times the work we do. Chiefs of Staff do confer. So do Service Ministers. P.M. has direct contact.' Here was an obverse side to Churchill's 'dictatorship': the confidence and efficiency his direct relations with service chiefs and Ministers inspired. It was this confidence which Menzies did not always recognise and which explains why, as Churchill's biographer, Martin Gilbert, has put it, 'increasingly as the war continued the War Cabinet was content to leave the conduct of the war to the Prime Minister and the Chiefs of Staff, and did not wish to be brought into strategic discussions'.[12]

Sometime soon after Menzies' return to Australia in 1941 he set down, in his neat, pencilled handwriting, his retrospective impressions of a number of the public men he had met and observed in action while abroad. He was obviously anxious to preserve his memories before they faded or were overlaid by the rush of wartime events. Perhaps, too, these little pieces were practice runs for the popular talks and broadcasts for which at this time Menzies was in great demand, or even exercises in codifying thoughts and honing phrases he would afterwards use in parliamentary speeches. The sketch of Churchill in this series is of particular importance in the light both of what we know about Churchill's relationship to his War Cabinet and of the ambivalent feelings about him which Menzies records day-to-day in his Diary. The very form of Menzies' appraisal catches at those ambivalences. It consists of carefully juxtaposed sizing-up statements organised around a series of perceived personal characteristics. As such, it captures the essence of Menzies' recent experiences, or rather of the emotions and judgements those experiences aroused, far more accurately than the memories he had, or thought he ought to have had, when so many years later he sat down to write *Afternoon Light*. By then, even his fragmentary understanding of the sources of Churchill's power seems to have quite faded.

---

11   Ibid., p. 324.
12   Ibid.

Churchill

1. Amazing command of English, with an unrivalled capacity for a striking phrase which will be quoted for days

1. But is liable to become the victim of his own phrase—which he will roll lovingly over his palate, with less and less criticism as the music of the phrase grows

2. The influence which this gives him over the spirit and ideas of the people

2. He conveys fighting courage, but makes no speeches with a lofty spiritual appeal

3. His real courage and fighting spirit, and unconquerable optimism

3. But engages in "wishful thinking" as to the facts. Inconvenient facts are frowned on & abolished with violence

4. His vast experience in affairs

4. But has no organising ability

5. He enjoys war and the conduct of war. It was his principal peace-time study

5. He therefore neglects entirely the economic, financial, social & industrial sides of war, which he leaves to others without more than spasmodic direction

6. He is greatly respected in USA and feared by Germany

6. But takes American support far too much for granted

7. Wherever he sends a cable or despatch, it is direct, forceful colloquial —a refreshing change from the F.O.

7. And yet frequently a less clever or biting phrase might have had a better result

8. Is clearly & beyond argument N° 1 in the Cabinet, and has unrivalled drive and energy

8. But takes care there shall be no N° 2 by completely suppressing by frown and attitude, all Cabinet discussions. There is no War Cabinet, and for other posts only yes-men need apply

9. Confers daily and intelligently with Chiefs of Staff, and has the most incredible knowledge of war detail

9. But no C/S stands up to him, or is allowed to. The amateur thus constantly overrules the professional, frequently without real argument from the pro

10. Is always fresh on the job. Takes a rest in bed every day after lunch

10. But breaks all the other rules of health. Smokes a cigar in bed before breakfast, stays up to 3am, likes drinking

11. Is a superb dinner table talker

11. But never listens to anybody else if he can help it

12. Is prepared (as is no other man except Beaverbrook) to cut through red tape and go out for results

12. But makes an erroneous exception in the case of his old favourite, the Admiralty, whose dock yard methods are hopeless, but which Winston defends because they were so "in Nelson's time"

13. Is always issuing spirited directives on the strategy of war, even to Generals in the field, and thus maintaining close and valuable contact

13. But forgets that conducting a campaign in the Middle East from Whitehall is not calculated to do much good in the long-run

14. Never spares himself. Will commence a Defence Committee meeting at 12 midnight

14. But forgets that Chiefs of Staff will have to get up at 7.30 next morning to get some of their ordinary work done. They are thus all overworked, tired, and to that extent inefficient

15. Has earned great and proper credit by making no speech of the "I told you so" order

15. But in conversation says unpardonable things about his predecessors, forgetting his own mistakes

Source: Undated, Menzies Family Papers.

SOURCES

For many points in our commentaries and footnotes we have drawn on the Papers of Sir Robert Menzies, held in the National Library of Australia, and on personal papers in the possession of the Menzies family, who kindly gave us permission to quote from both. Other primary references are acknowledged in the footnotes: it would be tedious, not to say pretentious, to list them in full here. Much was also drawn from the fully documented work *Robert Menzies: A Life*, vol. 1, *1894–1943* (Melbourne, 1993) by A.W. Martin assisted by Patsy Hardy.

For the identification of individuals we have used the standard biographical sources: *Australian Dictionary of Biography*, *The Dictionary of National Biography*, *Dictionary of American Biography*, various editions of *Who's Who*, *Who Was Who*, *Who's Who in Australia*, *Who's Who in America*, *The International Who's Who*, as well as *The British Imperial Calendar and Civil Service List*, and various Australian and British *Army*, *Navy* and *Air Force Lists*. On occasion, where these sources did not have the information we sought, we have obtained biographical details from: W.J. Hudson and H.W. Stokes (eds), *Documents on Australian Foreign Policy, 1937–49*. vol. IV: *July 1940–June 1941* (Canberra, 1980); John Colville, *The Fringes of Power: Downing Street Diaries 1939–1955* (Sevenoaks, 1986); and Gavin Long, *To Benghazi* (Canberra, 1952).

Some other, published, diaries for the same period as Menzies' are enlightening and entertaining: Colville, *Fringes of Power* (as listed above); David Dilks (ed), *The Diaries of Sir Alexander Cadogan O.M. 1938–1945* (London, 1971); Robert Rhodes James (ed), *Chips. The Diaries of Sir Henry Channon* (London, 1967); and Ben Pimlott (ed), *The Second World War Diary of Hugh Dalton 1940–45* (London, 1986).

Of the many useful secondary sources covering aspects of this period the following are particularly to be noted: Paul Hasluck, *The Government and the People, 1939–1941* (Canberra, 1952); Cameron Hazlehurst, *Menzies Observed* (Sydney, 1979); W.J. Hudson, *Casey* (Melbourne, 1986); Geoffrey Sawer, *Australian Federal Politics and Law, 1929–1949* (Melbourne, 1963); Gavin Souter, *Acts of Parliament* (Melbourne, 1988).

Works frequently cited have been identified by the following abbreviations

AA	Australian Archives
AWM	Australian War Memorial
Chips	Robert Rhodes James (ed), *Chips. The Diaries of Sir Henry Channon*
DAFP	W.J. Hudson and H.W. Stokes (eds), *Documents on Australian Foreign Policy, 1937–49*
Dalton	Ben Pimlott (ed), *The Second World War Diary of Hugh Dalton 1940–45*
Fringes	John Colville, *The Fringes of Power: Downing Street Diaries 1939–1955*
Hasluck	Paul Hasluck, *The Government and the People, 1939–1941*
Menzies Family Papers	Miscellaneous papers relating to the life and career of Sir Robert Menzies, held by the Menzies family
Menzies Film	Stills from the home movie taken by Menzies on his trip, courtesy of the Menzies family
Menzies 1935 Diary	Menzies 1935 Diary of his first trip to England, held in the Sir Robert Menzies Papers, National Library of Australia MS 4936, series 13
Menzies 1941 Diary	Menzies 1941 Diary held in the Sir Robert Menzies Papers, National Library of Australia MS 4936, series 13
Menzies Papers	Sir Robert Menzies Papers, National Library of Australia MS 4936, series 9
PRO CAB	Public Record Office, London. Cabinet Papers

INDEX

The index consists of references to names of people, countries and theatres of war.